REHABILITATIONS

and other Essays

REHABILITATIONS

AND OTHER ESSAYS

BY

CLIVE S. LEWIS, *1898-1963*.

Essay Index Reprint Series

BOOKS FOR LIBRARIES PRESS

FREEPORT, NEW YORK

First Published 1939
Reprinted 1972

Library of Congress Cataloging in Publication Data

Lewis, Clive Staples, 1898-1963.
    Rehabilitations, and other essays, by Clive S. Lewis. Freeport,
N.Y., Books for Libraries Pr. [1972]
    viii, 197 p. 23 cm.
    (Essay index reprint series)
    Reprint of the 1939 ed.
    CONTENTS:--Shelley, Dryden, and Mr. Eliot.--William
Morris.--The idea of an 'English school.'--[etc.]
    1. English literature--Addresses, essays, lectures.
I. Title.

PR99.L4 1972   820.9   71-167377
ISBN 0-8369-2559-9

PRINTED IN THE UNITED STATES OF AMERICA
BY
NEW WORLD BOOK MANUFACTURING CO., INC.
HALLANDALE, FLORIDA 33009

To

HUGO DYSON

PREFACE

A MAN is seldom moved to praise what he loves until it has been attacked. The first six essays in this book, which give it its title, were all in varying degrees provoked in this way. The first two defend great romantic poets against popular hatred or neglect of Romanticism. The third and fourth defend the present course of English studies at Oxford against certain criticisms; but so differently (the one having been addressed to a joint meeting of the Classical and English Associations and the other to undergraduates) that I hope they do not much overlap. The fifth is partly a defence of the many popular books which have, I believe, so greatly increased my power of enjoying more serious literature as well as 'real life'; but it is much more a defence of disinterested literary enjoyment in general against certain dangerous tendencies in modern education. I was afraid lest all the pleasant landscapes would soon be shut out by a wall of blackboards and 'certificates'. The sixth is perhaps a work of attack rather than of defence; but probably I should not have written it if I had not been stimulated by the contempt sometimes expressed for Anglo-Saxon poetry. It is here reprinted from *Lysistrata*.[1] In spite of the

[1] As far as I know this periodical did not survive my contribution, and I have been unable to discover the name and address of the lady who edited it. I hope that if these lines meet her eyes she will forgive me for assuming her permission to reprint.

apparent diversity of subject-matter, I like to think that the collection has a certain unity, in virtue of certain beliefs about life and books which are implicit throughout.

CONTENTS

I

SHELLEY, DRYDEN, AND MR. ELIOT

To heanlic me þinceþ
þæt ge mid urum sceattum to scype gangon
unbefohtene, nu ge þus feorr hider
in urne eard inn becomon

MALDON

Read at Bedford College, London

SHELLEY, DRYDEN, AND MR. ELIOT

FEW poets have suffered more than Shelley from
the modern dislike of the Romantics. It is natural
that this should be so. His poetry is, to an unusual
degree, entangled in political thought, and in a kind
of political thought now generally unpopular. His
belief in the natural perfectibility of man justly
strikes the Christian reader as foolishness; while, on
the other hand, the sort of perfection he has in view is
too ideal for dialectical materialists. His writings are
too generous for our cynics; his life is too loose for our
'humanist' censors. Almost every recent movement
of thought in one way or another serves to discredit
him. From some points of view, this reaction cannot
be regarded as wholly unfortunate. There is much
in Shelley's poetry that has been praised to excess;
much even that deserves no praise at all. In his
metre, with all its sweetness, there is much ignoble
fluidity, much of mere jingle. His use of language is
such that he seldom attains for long to the highest
qualities of distinction, and often sinks to a facility
and commonplace almost Byronic. He is not a *safe*
poet; you cannot open his works to refute one of his
enemies with any sense of confidence. But reaction
must not be allowed to carry us too far; and when
Mr. Eliot offers up Shelley as a sacrifice to the fame
of Dryden it is time to call a halt. To be sure, Mr.
Eliot has his own purpose in that comparison: he is
combating the view of the last century that Shelley
must necessarily be a greater poet than Dryden because his subjects are more obviously poetical—

because the one writes lyrics and the other satire, because one is in the coffee-house and the other in the clouds.[1] But we must not fall over, like Luther's drunk man, on the other side of the horse. Those who prefer Shelley to Dryden need not do so on the grounds which Mr. Eliot has envisaged; and to prove this I will now maintain that Shelley is to be regarded, on grounds which Mr. Eliot himself will allow, as a more masterly, a more sufficient, and indeed a more *classical* poet than Dryden.

The days are, or ought to be, long past in which any well-informed critic could take the couplet poets of our 'Augustan' school at their own valuation as 'classical' writers. This would be quite as grave an error as the romantic criticism which denied them to be men of genius. They are neither bad poets nor classical poets. Their merits are great, but neither their merits nor their limitations are those of ancient literature or of that modern literature which is truly classical. It would be hard to find any excellence in writing less classical than wit; yet it is in wit that these poets admittedly excel. The very forms in which the greatest and most characteristic of classical poetry is cast—the epic and the tragedy—are the forms which they attempt with least success. Their favourite form is Satire, a form not invented by the Greeks, and even in Roman hands not very like *Mac Fleknoe* or the *Dunciad*. But it is needless to labour the point. To any one who still thinks Pope a classical poet we can only say 'Open your Sophocles, your Virgil, your Racine, your Milton'; and if that experi-

[1] *Selected Essays*, 1932, p. 295.

ment does not convince him, we may safely dismiss him for a blockhead.

Of the school in general, then, we may say that it is a good, unclassical school. But when we turn to Dryden, we must, I think, say more than this. We must admit that we have here a great, flawed poet, in whom the flaws, besides being characteristically unclassical, are scarcely forgivable even by the most romantic or revolutionary standards.

I have said 'a great, flawed poet'. Of the greatness I wish to make no question; and it is a greatness to which the name of *genius* is peculiarly applicable. The most abiding impression which Dryden makes upon us is that of exuberant power. He is what Middle English critics would have called 'boisteous'. He excels in beginnings. 'A milk white hind immortal and unchanged'—'In pious times ere priestcraft did begin'—there is no fumbling at the exordium. He leaps into his first paragraph as an athlete leaps into the hundred yards' track, and before the fascination of his ringing couplets gives us leisure to take breath we have been carried into the heart of his matter. The famous 'magnanimity' of his satire is another aspect of this same quality of power. His strength is so great that he never needs—or never gives us the impression of needing—to use it all. He is justly praised by Mr. Eliot for 'what he has made of his material', for his 'ability to make the small into the great, the prosaic into the poetic':[1] not that the value of a literary result is in a direct ratio to its difficulty— a theory with absurd consequences—but that the

[1] Op. cit., p. 296.

sheer strength of the poet is more easily judged when it is thus isolated. Of this transforming power I know no better example than the résumé of the political situation which opens *Absalom and Achitophel*. Not only is the prosaic made poetical, but the obscure and complicated is made clear and simple. A child can hardly fail to understand the state of Israel as Dryden describes it; and yet surprisingly little of that situation, as Dryden saw it, has been omitted. If anything is misrepresented, the misrepresentation is deliberate.

Mr. Eliot himself selects, to illustrate this transforming power, a passage from *Alexander's Feast* and another from *Cymon and Iphigenia*. The first is that in which the tipsy Alexander 'Fought all his battles o'er again; And thrice he routed all his foes, and thrice he slew the slain'. Certainly, if the thing was to be done at all, this is the way to do it. The sudden irruption of the country-dancing fourteener among the nobler, if never very subtle, rhythms of the ode, most happily expresses the transition from heroics to a tavern scene. Dryden has brought off his effect—and it is an effect which will be dear to all who hate the heroic and cannot see any civil or religious ceremony without wishing that some one may slip. For a critic like Mr. Eliot, however, the question must surely be not only whether a given effect has been attained, but also whether, and why, it ought to have been attempted. Certain classicists would resent the intrusion of the comic into the greater ode at all, as an offence against decorum. I am sure that Mr. Eliot remembers, and almost sure he approves, the delicious reproaches levelled against Racine by French critics for venturing within the remotest hailing distance of comedy in certain scenes of *Andromaque*; and the greater ode is as lofty a form as tragedy. But even if we allow the comic note, can we excuse comedy of quite this hackneyed and heavy-handed type? That Alexander in his cups should resemble exactly the first drunken braggart whom you may meet in a railway refreshment room, appears to Mr. Eliot to add 'a delicate flavour'.[1] But what is there delicate about it? Indelicacy, in the sense of grossness and crudity of apprehension, ἀγροικία, is surely the very essence of it. It does not seem to have crossed Dryden's mind that when Alexander got drunk he may have behaved like a drunk gentleman or a drunk scholar and not like an 'old soldier'. No: this is not a subtle or delicate joke. If it is to be defended at all, it must be defended as a 'good plain joke'. As such, Mr. Eliot apparently likes it, and I do not: and this is of very little consequence. What is important is that the passage raises in our minds a rather disturbing doubt about Dryden's poetical purity of intention. The joke may be good or bad in itself. Let us suppose that it is good;—the question remains whether even a good joke, of this tavern type, really contributes to the total effect of the ode. Does Dryden really care whether it contributes or not? Is he, in fine, a man ready, for every ray of accidental beauty that may come in his way, to sacrifice the integrity of his work —a dabbler in 'good passages'—a man who can produce good poetry but not good poems?

---

[1] Op. cit., p. 297.

As regards *Alexander's Feast* I am content to leave the question open: when once it has been raised we shall have no difficulty in answering it for the rest of Dryden's more considerable works. What do we enjoy in *Absalom and Achitophel*? Undoubtedly, the incidental merits. Of the poëm taken as a whole, as a ποίημα, Johnson has said the last word.

'There is an unpleasing disproportion between the beginning and the end. We are alarmed by a faction formed of many sects, various in their principles, but agreeing in their purpose of mischief, formidable for their numbers, and strong by their supports; while the King's friends are few and weak. The chiefs on either part are set forth to view: but when expectation is at the height, the King makes a speech, and
       Henceforth a series of new times began.'

No doubt, the very nature of the case compelled Dryden to this fault; but that excuses the man without mending the poem. I do not argue *why* the work is botched, but *that* it is. It is even part of my case that the defect in *Absalom* was unavoidable. It is a radical defect, consubstantial with Dryden's original conception. It is no mere accident. The work is not merely maimed, it is diseased at the heart. Like many human invalids, it is not lacking in charms and happy moments; but classicists like Mr. Eliot (and myself) should not accept any amount of littered poetry as a poem. If we turn to the *Hind and the Panther* we find the same irredeemable defect in an aggravated form. Of course it is full of 'good things'; but of the plan itself, the nerve and structure of the poem, what are we to say if not that the very design

of conducting in verse a theological controversy alle-
gorized as a beast fable suggests in the author a state
of mind bordering on aesthetic insanity? If the poet
had succeeded it would indeed provide a noble example of the transforming power which Mr. Eliot
claims for him. But he has not. *The Hind and the
Panther* does not exist, as *Phèdre* or *Persuasion* or *The
Alchemist* exist. It is not a poem: it is simply a name
which we give for convenience to a number of pieces
of good description, vigorous satire, and 'popular'
controversy, which have all been yoked together by
external violence.

It may be objected that I am selecting poems
merely occasional, specimens at least of 'applied'
poetry, which cannot fairly be judged by the highest
standards. But this is dangerous argument for the
defenders of Dryden. The two poems I have quoted
are among his most considerable works: they contain
much of his noblest, and much of his most piquant,
poetry. If these have to be thrown to the wolves as
mere applied poetry for which special indulgence is
sued, it will be hard, on what remains, to support the
plea that Dryden is a poet comparable to Shelley.
But I pass over this difficulty. Let us turn to works
more purely 'poetical', and specially to the *Fables*
which no one asked him to write. Here, if anywhere,
we may hope to find the real 'maker' at last instead
of the mere fountain of brilliant 'passages'. Here,
perhaps, Dryden will become the master, not the
slave, of inspiration.

It falls out very happily that Mr. Eliot should have
chosen from one of these fables a passage in illustra-

to tell a tragic and 'heroic' story. It is not a story of
the highest order. It suffers from that overstrain and
tendency to falsetto which is the infallible mark of
the prosaic mind desperately determined to be
'poetical'. You could not make an *Oedipus* or a *Lear*
out of it; you might make a *Cid*. But it is, at least, a
story worth telling. And now mark what Dryden
does with it. He does not intend to forgo a single
thrill of the tragic ending. He intends to purge our
emotions. We are to see the heroine 'devoutly glue'
her lips to the heart of her murdered husband, and
our respect is to be demanded for her 'Mute solemn
sorrow without female noise'. That is the note on
which the poem is to end. And yet, with such an end
in view, this old poet goes out of his way to insert at
the beginning of his story a ribald picture of his
heroine as the lascivious widow of conventional
comedy. I will not quote the pitiful lines in which
Dryden winks and titters to his readers over these
time-honoured salacities. The reader may turn to
the passage for himself. And when he has read on
to the bitter end of it, to that couplet where even
Dryden's skill in language deserts him and we sink
to the scribbled meanness of

> On either side the kisses flew so thick
> That neither she nor he had breath to speak,

then let him remind himself that all this is the beginning of a tragic story, and that Dryden will presently
try to make sublime this same woman whom he is
here turning into a Widow Wadman. For such sin
against the essential principles of all poetry whatever,
no excuse can be made. It cannot be accident.

Dryden is the most conscious of writers: he knows well what he is doing. He destroys, and is content to destroy, the kind of poem he sat down to write, if only he can win in return one guffaw from the youngest and most graceless of his audience. There is in this a poetic blasphemy, an arrogant contempt for his own art, which cannot, I think, be paralleled in any other great writer.

It would show a serious misunderstanding if Dryden's partisans pleaded at this point that I was enslaved to some Victorian canon of solemnity as the essence of poetry and judging Dryden by an alien standard. I have no quarrel with comic or cynical or even ribald poetry. I have no quarrel with Wycherley, I admire Congreve, I delight in Prior and still more in *Don Juan*. I delight in Dryden himself when he is content to talk bawdy in season and consider 'Sylvia the fair in the bloom of fifteen' a very pretty piece. But in these fables—as also in the heroic tragedies which are similarly blemished—it is Dryden, not I, who has chosen that the heroic should be trumps, and has lost the game by rules of his own choosing. It was Dryden, not I, who decided to write *Annus Mirabilis* as a serious and lofty historical poem on what he regarded as the 'successes of a most just and necessary war'. If, after that decision, he describes the enemy as

Vast bulks which little souls but ill supply,

then we have every right to tell that a nation of reasonable men, not to say men of courage and honour, are very ill-celebrated by the insinuation that their enemies are lubbers. This kind of thing

runs through all Dryden's attempts at the graver and
more enthusiastic kinds of poetry, and it must be
remembered that such attempts make up a large part
of his work. The sin is so flagrant that I cannot
understand how so cultivated a critic as Mr. Eliot has
failed to see the truth; which truth had now better be
stated quite frankly. Dryden fails to be a satisfactory
poet because being rather a boor, a gross, vulgar,
provincial, misunderstanding mind, he yet constantly
attempts those kinds of poetry which demand the
cuor gentil. Like so many men of that age he is deeply
influenced by the genuinely aristocratic and heroic
poetry of France. He admires the world of the French
tragedians—that exalted tableland where rhetoric
and honour grow naturally out of the life lived and
the culture inherited. We in England had had an
aristocratic tradition of our own, to be sure; a tradition at once more sober and more tenderly romantic
than the French, obeying a code of honour less dis-
sociated from piety. The Duke and Duchess of New-
castle were perhaps its last exponents. But Dryden
seems to know nothing of it. He and his audiences
look to Versailles, and feel for it that pathetic yet
unprofitable yearning which vulgarity so often feels
for unattainable graces. But the yearning does not
teach them the secret. Where their model was brilliant they are flashy; where the *Cid* was brave,
Almansor swaggers; refinements of amorous casuistry
out of the heroic romances are aped by the loves of
grooms and chambermaids. One is reminded of a
modern oriental, who may have the blood of old
paynim knighthoods in him, but who prefers to

dress himself up as a cheap imitation of a European gentleman.

The worst thing about such challenging praise as Mr. Eliot offers Dryden—praise, I believe, with which Dryden would be seriously embarrassed—is that it forces the rest of us to remember Dryden's faults. I have dealt with them, as I see them, plainly, not maliciously. The man is irremediably ignorant of that world he chooses so often to write about. When he confines himself to satire, he is at home; but even here, the fatal lack of architectonic power seldom allows him to make a satisfactory poem. That is the case against Dryden. It would have been pleasanter to state the case for him—to analyse, in order to praise, the masculine vigour of his English, the fine breezy, sunshiny weather of the man's mind at its best—his poetical health; the sweetness (unsurpassed in its own way) of nearly all his versification. But we cannot allow him to be used, and so used, as a stick to beat Shelley.

I have now to show that Shelley, with all his faults of execution, is a poet who must rank higher than Dryden with any critic who claims to be classical; that he is superior to Dryden by the greatness of his subjects and his moral elevation (which are merits by classical standards), and also by the unity of his actions, his architectonic power, and his general observance of *decorum* in the Renaissance sense of the word; that is, his disciplined production not just of poetry but of the poetry in each case proper to the theme and the species of composition. But it is hardly possible in the present age to approach these questions without first removing some popular prejudices.

In the first place there is the prejudice which leads many people to mutter the word 'Godwin' as soon as Shelley is mentioned. They are quite sure that Godwin wrote a very silly book; they are quite sure that the philosophic content of much Shelleyan poetry is Godwinian; and they conclude that the poetry must be silly too. Their first premiss I cannot discuss, since a regrettable gap in my education has left me still the only critic in England who has not that familiar knowledge of *Political Justice* which alone can justify confident adverse criticism. But the second I can.[1] It is quite clear to any reader of general education—it must be clear, for example, to Mr. Eliot—that the influence of Dante and Plato is at least as dominant in Shelley's thought as that of Godwin—unless, indeed, Godwin shared the opinions of Dante and Plato, in which case Godwin cannot have been so very silly. Thus, I do not know what Godwin says about free love; but I see that the passage in *Epipsychidion* beginning

True love in this differs from gold and clay

may well derive from *Purgatorio* xv. 49, and thus ultimately from Aristotle's *Ethics* 1169 A. I do not myself agree with Shelley's application of the doctrine to sexual promiscuity; but then Plato, and many communists, would, and neither Shelley nor Godwin

[1] It will be noticed that even if the premises were true, the inference is invalid. A similar paralogism has occurred about Mr. Housman (of course, since his death) in the form, 'Kipling is bad. Some lines of Housman are like some lines of Kipling. Therefore Housman is bad.'

need be made the scapegoat. Thus again, in *Prometheus Unbound* I see that the main theme—the myth of a universal rebirth, a restoration of all things—is one which may occur in any age and which falls naturally into place beside Isaiah or the Fourth Eclogue, and that to pin it down to Godwin is a provincialism. Something it may owe to Godwin; but its debts to Aeschylus and, as Mr. Tillyard has shown, to Plato's *Politicus* are at least equally interesting. If Shelley were an ignoramus who had read no book but *Political Justice*, or a dullard who could invent nothing, we might be driven to suppose that his Asia was merely a personification of Godwinian benevolence; but when we know that he had read of divine love and beauty in Plato and remember that he wrote the *Hymn to Intellectual Beauty*, the identification becomes merely perverse. And finally, whatever Godwin may really have said, one of the chief tenets attributed to him is explicitly rejected at the end of Act III. Let us hear no more of Godwin.[1]

Another prejudice is harder to combat because it is ill-defined. It usually expresses itself by the damning epithet 'adolescent'; it began with Arnold's phrase about the 'ineffectual angel'. Shelley is supposed to be not merely *seely* in the Elizabethan sense, but *silly* in the modern sense; to believe ludicrously well of the human heart in general, and crudely ill of a few tyrants; to be, in a word, insufficiently disillusioned. Before removing this misunderstanding,

---

[1] That is, nothing more in the usual strain. For a reprint of *Political Justice* (a book very difficult to find) I am all agog: it is not likely to be so dull as our critical tradition proclaims.

I must point out that if it were granted it would not place him below Dryden. Dryden is equally ignorant of the world, though in the opposite direction, as his sorry joke about Alexander would be sufficient to show. Whenever he attempts to be lofty he betrays himself. There are senile and vulgar illusions no less than illusions adolescent and heroical; and of the two, I see no reason for preferring the former. If I must, in either event, be blindfold, why should I choose to have my eyes bandaged with stinking clouts rather than with cloth of gold? The fashion indeed is all for the stinking clouts, and it is easy to see why. Men (and, still more, boys) like to call themselves disillusioned because the very form of the word suggests that they have had the illusions and emerged from them—have tried both worlds. The claim, however, is false in nine cases out of ten. The world is full of impostors who claim to be disenchanted and are really unenchanted: mere 'natural' men who have never risen so high as to be in danger of the generous illusions they claim to have escaped from. Mr. Mencken is the perfect example. We need to be on our guard against such people. They talk like sages who have passed through the half-truths of humanitarian benevolence, aristocratic honour, or romantic passion, while in fact they are clods who have never yet advanced so far. 'Ἀπειροκαλία is their disease; and Dryden himself is not free from it. He has not escaped from those enchantments which some find in Shelley; he has tried desperately to taste the like, and failed, and the fustian remains in his poetry like a scar on his face. He indeed deserves pity, since he has struggled against the disease, unlike our modern impostors who glory in it and call it health; but this does not alter the conclusion that he cannot be set against Shelley as one who knows against one who is deluded. If we granted the doctrine of Shelley's amiable ignorance of the one half of life, it would still but balance Dryden's banausic ignorance of the other.

But I do not grant the doctrine, and I do not see how it can be accepted by any one who has read Shelley's poetry with attention. It is simply not true to say that Shelley conceives the human soul as a naturally innocent and divinely beautiful creature, interfered with by external tyrants. On the contrary no other heathen writer comes nearer to stating and driving home the doctrine of original sin. In such an early work as *The Revolt of Islam* those who come 'from pouring human blood' are told to

Disguise it not—we have one human heart—
All mortal thoughts confess a common home. (VIII. xix.)

and again,

>   Look on your mind—it is the book of fate—
>   Ah! it is dark with many a blazoned name
>   Of misery—*all are mirrors of the same.* (xx.)

This is weak, exclamatory poetry, I grant you, but my concern is with the *sentens*. When Shelley looks at and condemns the oppressor he does so with the full consciousness that he also is a man just like that: the evil is within as well as without; all are wicked, and this of course is the significance of the allegorical

passage in *Prometheus Unbound*, where the Furies say
to Prometheus

> We will live through thee, one by one,
> Like animal life, and though we can obscure not
> The soul which burns within, that we will dwell
> Beside it, like a vain loud multitude
> Vexing the self-content of wisest men:
> That we will be dread thought beneath thy brain
> And foul desire round thine astonished heart,
> And blood within thy labyrinthine veins
> Crawling like agony.
> *Prom.*   Why ye are thus now.

The same doctrine, more briefly and suggestively
expressed, occurs in the *Triumph of Life*, where he
explains the failure of the wise, the great, and the
unforgotten by saying

>   their lore
> Taught them not this, to know themselves; their might
> Could not repress *the mystery within.*
> And for the morn of truth they feigned, deep night
> Caught them ere evening. (211–15.)

We mistake Shelley wholly if we do not understand
that for him, as certainly as for St. Paul, humanity in
its merely natural or 'given' condition is a body of
death. It is true that the conclusion he draws is very
different from that of St. Paul. To a Christian, conviction of sin is a good thing because it is the necessary
preliminary to repentance; to Shelley it is an extremely dangerous thing. It begets self-contempt,
and self-contempt begets misanthropy and cruelty.
In the *Revolt of Islam* the passage I have already
quoted leads up to the statement that it is this self-
contempt which arms Hatred with a 'mortal sting'.

The man who has once seen the darkness within himself will soon seek vengeance on others; and in *Prometheus* self-contempt is twice mentioned as an evil. I do not think we can seriously doubt that Shelley is right. If a man will not become a Christian, it is very undesirable that he should become aware of the reptilian inhabitants in his own mind. To know how bad we are, in the condition of mere nature, is an excellent recipe for becoming much worse. The process is very accurately described in some of the most memorable lines Shelley ever wrote:

> 'Tis a trick of this same family
> To analyse their own and other minds.
> Such self-anatomy shall teach the will
> Dangerous secrets: for it *tempts our powers,*
> *Knowing what must be thought and may be done,*
> Into the depth of darkest purposes:
> So Cenci fell into the pit; even I
> Since Beatrice *unveiled me to myself,*
> *And made me shrink from what I cannot shun,*
> *Show a poor figure to my own esteem,*
> *To which I grow half reconciled.* . . .
>
> (Cenci, II. ii. 108 et seq.)

The lines which I have italicized provide an excellent short history of thought and sentiment in the early twentieth century, and the whole passage is a measure of the difference between Byron and Shelley. Byron, speaking through his Byronic heroes, is in the very article of that process which Shelley describes, and rather proud of it. He suffers the predicament; Shelley observes and understands it. He understands it, I think, a good deal better than most of his modern critics.

Shelley's poetry presents a variety of kinds, most of them traditional. The elegy and the greater ode come down to him from the *exemplaria graeca* through eighteenth-century practice; the metrical structure of the latter is indeed rooted in a misunderstanding of Pindar, but a misunderstanding which had become itself a precedent by Shelley's time. *Swellfoot* is almost an attempt to revive the Old Comedy—an attempt which should interest Mr. Eliot since Shelley in it faces the cardinal problem of much of Mr. Eliot's poetry: namely, whether it is possible to distinguish poetry about squalor and chaos from squalid and chaotic poetry. I do not think it a great success. The lyrical drama is in part Aeschylean; in part, I think, Shelley's redemption of a bad eighteenth-century form. It derives from, and redeems, the drama of Mason, just as *The Prelude* and *Excursion* derive from, and confer new power upon, the eighteenth-century treatise-poem. Shelley's lyric is a greater novelty, but heavily indebted on the metrical side to Dryden himself. The fantastic tale or idyll (as in *Alastor* or the *Witch of Atlas*) probably derives from the mythological epyllion of the Elizabethans. In all these kinds Shelley produces works which, though not perfect, are in one way more satisfactory than any of Dryden's longer pieces: that is to say, they display a harmony between the poet's real and professed intention, they answer the demands of their forms, and they have unity of spirit. Shelley is at home in his best poems, his clothes, so to speak, fit him, as Dryden's do not. The faults are faults of execution, such as over-elaboration, occasional verbosity, and the like: mere stains on the surface. The faults in Dryden are fundamental discrepancies between the real and the assumed poetic character, or radical vices in the design: diseases at the heart. Shelley could almost say with Racine, 'When my plan is made my poem is done'; with Dryden the plan itself usually foredooms the poem's failure.

Thus *Alastor* is a poem perfectly true to itself. The theme is universally interesting—the quest for ideal love. And both the theme and the treatment are fully suited to Shelley's powers. Hence the poem has an apparent ease, a noble obviousness, which deceives some readers. Mr. Eliot himself is too experienced a writer to be guilty of the delusion that he could write like Shelley if he chose; but I think many of Mr. Eliot's readers may suffer from it. They mistake the inevitability of *Alastor*, which really springs from the poet's harmony with his subject, for the facility of commonplace, and condemn the poem precisely because it is successful. Of course it has its faults—some of the scenery is over-written, and the form of line which ends with two long monosyllables comes too often. But these are not the sort of defects that kill a poem: the energy of imagination, which supports so lofty, remote, and lonely an emotion almost without a false note for seven hundred lines, remains; and it deserves to be admired, if in no higher way, at least as we admire a great suspension-bridge. I address myself, of course, only to those who are prepared, by toleration of the theme, to let the poem have a fair hearing. For those who are not, we can only say that they may doubtless be very worthy

people, but they have no place in the European
tradition.

Perhaps this muscular sustaining power is even
more noticeable in the *Witch of Atlas*, for there Shelley
goes more out of himself. In *Alastor* the congeniality
of the theme was fully given in Shelley's temper; in
the *Witch* he is going successfully beyond the bounds
of his temper—making himself something other than
he was. For in this poem we have, indeed, Shelley's
ordinary romantic love of the fantastical and ideal,
but all keyed down, muted, deftly inhibited from its
native solemnity and intensity in order to produce a
lighter, more playful effect. The theme, at bottom,
is as serious as ever; but the handling 'turns all to
favour and to prettiness'. The lightness and liquidity
of this piece, the sensation which we feel in reading it
of seeing things distinctly, yet at a vast distance,
cannot be paralleled in any poem that I know. We
must go to another art, namely to music, to find anything at all similar; and there we shall hardly find it
outside Mozart. It could not, indeed, have been
written if Shelley had not read the Italians; but it is
a new modification, and in it all the light-hearted
dancing perfection of Ariosto is detached from
Ariosto's hardness and flippancy (though not from
his irony) and used with a difference—disturbed by
overtones, etherialized. The whole poem is a happy
reproof to that new Puritanism which has captured
so many critics and taught us to object to pleasure
in poetry simply because it is pleasure. It is natural,
though regrettable, that such people should be
exasperated by this mercurial poem; for to them

it is miching mallecho (as Shelley said of *Peter Bell*) and means, as so much of his poetry means, mischief. They know very well that they are being laughed at; and they do not like to be told how

> Heaven and Earth conspire to foil
> The over-busy gardener's blundering toil.

If Shelley had written only such poems he would have shown his genius: his artistry, the discipline and power of obedience which makes genius universal, are better shown elsewhere. *Adonais* naturally occurs to the mind, for here we see Shelley fruitfully submitting to the conventions of a well-established form. It has all the traditional features of the elegy—the opening dirge, the processional allegory, and the concluding consolation. There is one bad error of taste. The Muse, lamenting Adonais, is made to lament her own immortality,

> I would give
> All that I am to be as thou now art!
> But I am chained to Time, and cannot thence depart.
> (XXVI.)

This is to make a goddess speak like a new-made human widow, and to dash the public solemnity of elegy with the violent passions of a personal lyric. How much more fitting are the words of the Roman poet:

> Immortales mortales flere si foret fas,
> Flerent divae Camenae Naevium poetam.

But it is a slip soon recovered, and not to be compared with the prolonged indecorum of Dryden's satiric conceits in his elegy for Mrs. Anne Killigrew:

> To the next realm she stretch'd her sway
> For Painture near adjoining lay

A plenteous province, and alluring prey.
　A chamber of Dependencies was fram'd
(As conquerors will never want pretence,
　When arm'd, to justify th' offence)
And the whole fief, in right of poetry, she claim'd.
The country open lay without defence, &c.

There are eighteen lines of it, and I do not know whether any major poet other than Dryden ever played such silly tricks at a funeral. No one demands that every poet should write an elegy: let each man be a master of his own trade. But the fact remains that when Shelley intends to do so, he does so; Dryden, equally intending, does not—*nimium amator ingenii sui*. I do not now speak of the unexampled rapture of Shelley's close. I might do so if I were to argue with Dryden, for he loves this ecstasy and quotes with approval *furentis animi vaticinatio*; being often a romantic in wish, though seldom happily romantic in the event. But I do not know whether Mr. Eliot shares Dryden's admiration for 'those enthusiastic parts of poetry'; and I would prefer to argue from positions that are, or ought in logic to be, admitted by Mr. Eliot. But I have slipped into that sentence 'If I were to argue with Dryden' unawares. Let no one suppose I am such a coxcomb as to think that my defence of Shelley could stand against Dryden's humane and luminous and Olympian dialectic; or, indeed, that it would be required in the presence of one who would almost certainly shame and antici- pate me with such generous praise of Shelley as he has given to Shakespeare, or Milton, or Tasso, and a frank acknowledgement (he made more than one) of his own offences against the laws of poetry. Whoever else is a Drydenian in Mr. Eliot's way, I have no fear lest Dryden himself should be one.

Of course Shelley too had his failures. The *Revolt of Islam* does not really exist much more than the *Hind and the Panther* exists, and the ruin is less redeemed by fine passages. The *Letter to Maria Gisborne* is little better than a draft—a thing scrawled as quickly as the pen would cover the paper and really unfit for the printer. *Peter Bell the Third* is a more doubtful case. I am not prepared to endure either its squalors or its obscurity by any such moderate promise of enjoyment as it holds out; but perhaps the creator of Sweeney ought to have more patience both with the one and with the other. I do not greatly admire—but perhaps some of Mr. Eliot's weaker disciples should—this little picture:

> As he was speaking came a spasm
>   And wrenched his gnashing teeth asunder:
> Like one who sees a strange phantasm
> He lay—there was a silent chasm
>   Between his upper jaw and under.

Epipsychidion raises in an acute form a problem with which Mr. Eliot has been much occupied: I mean the problem of the relation between our judgement on a poem as critics, and our judgement as men on the ethics, metaphysics, or theology presupposed or expressed in the poem. For my own part, I do not believe that the poetic value of any poem is identical with the philosophic; but I think they can differ only to a limited extent, so that every poem whose prosaic or intellectual basis is silly, shallow, perverse, or illiberal, or even radically erroneous, is in some degree crippled by that fact. I am thus obliged to rate *Epipsychidion* rather low, because I consider the thought implied in it a dangerous delusion. In it Shelley is trying to stand on a particular rung of the Platonic ladder, and I happen to believe firmly that that particular rung does not exist, and that the man who thinks he is standing on it is not standing but falling. But no view that we can adopt will remove *Epipsychidion* from the slate. There is an element of spiritual, and also of carnal, passion in it, each expressed with great energy and sensibility, and the whole is marred, but not completely, by the false mode (as Mr. Eliot and I would maintain) in which the poet tries to blend them. It is particularly interesting to notice the internal, perhaps unconscious, control which arises amidst the very intensity of the experience and tightens up the metrical form: the first forty lines are almost 'stopped couplets' and the whole movement is much closer to Dryden's couplet than to that of Keats.

But we are now rapidly approaching that part of our subject where the difference between Mr. Eliot and myself ceases. In his essay on Dante, Mr. Eliot says that he thinks the last canto of the *Paradiso* 'the highest point that poetry has ever reached'.[1] I think the same—and since it is so pleasant to agree, let me add irrelevantly that I think as he does about the *Bhagavad-Gita*.[2] And a few pages later Mr. Eliot singles Shelley out as the one English poet of his century (I would have said the one English poet yet

[1] Op. cit., p. 227.　　　　[2] Op. cit., p. 244.

recorded) 'who could even have begun to follow'
Dante's footsteps;[1] and he generously allows that
Shelley, at the end of his life, was beginning to profit
by his knowledge of Dante. I do not know how much
of Shelley's work Mr. Eliot would admit by this con-
cession. I suppose he would admit, at the very least,
the *Triumph of Life*. If any passage in our poetry has
profited by Dante, it is the unforgettable appearance
of Rousseau in that poem—though admittedly it is
only the Dante of the *Inferno*. But I am not without
hope that Mr. Eliot might be induced to include
more. In this same essay he speaks of a modern
'prejudice against beatitude as material for poetry'.[2]
Now Dante is eminently the poet of beatitude. He
has not only no rival, but none second to him. But
if we were asked to name the poet who most nearly
deserved this inaccessible *proxime accessit*, I should
name Shelley. Indeed, my claim for Shelley might
be represented by the proposition that Shelley and
Milton are, each, the half of Dante. I do not know
how we could describe Dante better to one who had
not read him, than by some such device as the following:

'You know the massive quality of Milton, the sense that
every word is being held in place by a gigantic pressure,
so that there is an architectural sublime in every verse
whether the matter be sublime at the moment or not.
You know also the air and fire of Shelley, the very antithesis of the Miltonic solidity, the untrammelled, reckless
speed through pellucid spaces which makes us imagine
while we are reading him that we have somehow left our
bodies behind. If now you can imagine (but you cannot,

[1] Op. cit., p. 250.   [2] Ibid.

for it must seem impossible till you see it dóne) a poetry
which combined these two all-but incompatibles—a poetry
as bright and piercing and aereal as the one, yet as weighty,
as pregnant and as lapidary as the other, then you will
know what Dante is like.'

To be thus half of Dante (Caesar is my authority for
such a rarefied critical symbolism) is fame enough for
any ordinary poet. And Shelley, I contend, reaches
this height in the fourth act of *Prometheus*.

Genetically considered, the fourth act, we know,
is an afterthought: teleologically it is that for which
the poem exists. I do not mean by this that the three
preceding acts are mere means; but that their significance and beauty are determined by what follows,
and that what came last in the writing (as it comes
last in the reading) is 'naturally prior' in the Aristotelian sense. It does not add to, and therefore corrupt,
a completed structure; it gives structure to that
which, without it, would be imperfect. The resulting
whole is the greatest long poem in the nineteenth
century, and the only long poem of the highest kind
in that century which approaches to perfection.

The theme is one of sane, public, and perennial
interest—that of rebirth, regeneration, the new cycle.
Like all great myths its primary appeal is to the
imagination: its indirect and further appeal to the
will and the understanding can therefore be diversely
interpreted according as the reader is a Christian, a
politician, a psycho-analyst, or what not. Myth is
thus like manna; it is to each man a different dish and
to each the dish he needs. It does not grow old nor
stick at frontiers racial, sexual, or philosophic; and

even from the same man at the same moment it can
elicit different responses at different levels. But great
myth is rare in a reflective age; the temptation to
allegorize, to thrust into the story the conscious
doctrines of the poet, there to fight it out as best they
can with the inherent tendency of the fable, is usually
too strong. *Faust* and the *Niblung's Ring*—the only
.other great mythical poems of modern times—have
in this way been partially spoiled. The excellence of
Shelley is that he has avoided this. He has found
what is, for him, the one perfect story and re-made
it so well that the ancient version now seems merely
embryonic. In his poem there is no strain between
the literal sense and the imaginative significance.
The events which are needed to produce the λύσις
seem to become the symbols of the spiritual process
he is presenting without effort or artifice or even
consciousness on his part.

The problem was not an easy one. We are to start
with the soul chained, aged, suffering; and we are to
end with the soul free, rejuvenated, and blessed. The
selection of the Prometheus story (a selection which
seems obvious only because we did not have to make
it) is the first step to the solution. But nearly everything has still to be done. By what steps are we to
pass from Prometheus in his chains to Prometheus
free? The long years of his agony cannot be dramatically represented, for they are static. The actual
moment of liberation by Heracles is a mere piece of
'business'. Dramatic necessity demands that the
Titan himself should do or say something before his
liberation—and if possible something that will have

an effect on the action. Shelley answers this by
beginning with Prometheus's revocation of the curse
upon Jupiter. Now mark how everything falls into
place for the poet who well and truly obeys his
imagination. This revocation at once introduces the
phantasm of Jupiter, the original curse on the phantasm's lips, and the despair of Earth and Echoes at
what seems to be Prometheus's capitulation. We
thus get at one stroke a good opening episode and a
fine piece of irony, on the dramatic level; but we also
have suggested the phantasmal or nightmare nature
of the incubus under which the soul (or the world) is
groaning, and the prime necessity for a change of
heart in the sufferer, who is in some sort his own
prisoner. Prometheus, we are made to feel, has really
stepped out of prison with the words, 'It doth repent
me.' But once again structural and spiritual necessities join hands to postpone his effective liberation.
On the structural side, the play must go on; on the
other, we know, and Shelley knows, how long a
journey separates the first resolve, from the final
remaking, of a man, a nation, or a world. The Furies
will return, and the act closes with low-toned melo-
dies of sadness and of hopes that are as yet remote
and notional.

The whole of the next act, in story, is occupied with
the difficult efforts of Asia to apprehend and follow a
dream dreamed in the shadow of Prometheus: the
difficult journey which it leads her; her difficult
descent to the depths of the earth; and her final reascension, transformed, to the light. Difficulty is, so
to speak, the subject of this act. The dramatic advan-

tage of splitting the sufferer's role into two parts, those of Prometheus and Asia, and of giving the latter a task to perform in the liberation, is sufficiently obvious. But we hardly need to notice this. Most of us, while we read this act, are too absorbed, I fancy, by the new sensation it creates in us. The gradual ineluctable approach of the unknown, where the unknown is sinister, is not an uncommon theme in literature; but where else are we to find this more medicinable theme—these shy approaches, and sudden recessions, and returnings beyond hope, and swellings and strengthenings of a far-off, uncertainly prognosticated good? And again, it is a necessity for Shelley, simply because he has placed his fiend in the sky, to make Asia go down, not up, to fetch this good; but how miraculously it all fits in! Does any reader, whether his prepossessions be psychological or theological, question this descent into hell, this return to the womb, this death, as the proper path for Asia to take? Our imaginations, constrained by deepest necessities, accept all that imagery of interwoven trees and dew and moss whereby the chorus drench the second scene with darkness, and the softness and damp of growing things: by the same necessity they accept the harsher images of the final precipitous descent to Demogorgon's cave, and the seated darkness which we find there. It is out of all this, silver against this blackness, that the piercing song of Asia's reascension comes; and if any one who has read that song in its setting still supposes that the poet is talking about Godwin or the Revolution, or that Shelley is any other than a very great poet, I cannot help him.

But for my own part I believe that no poet has felt more keenly, or presented more weightily the necessity for a complete unmaking and remaking of man, to be endured at the dark bases of his being. I do not know the book (in profane literature) to which I should turn for a like expression of what von Hügel would have called the 'costingness' of regeneration.

The third act is the least successful: Shelley's error was not to see that he could shorten it when once he had conceived the fourth. Yet some leisure and some slackened tension are here allowable. We are certainly not ready for the fourth act at once. Between the end of torment and the beginning of ecstasy there must be a pause: peace comes before beatitude. It would be ridiculous, in point of achievement, to compare this weak act in Shelley's play with the triumphant conclusion of the *Purgatorio*; but structurally it corresponds to the position of the earthly paradise between purgatory and heaven. And in one scene at least it is worthy of its theme. The dialogue between Ocean and Apollo (at 'the mouth of a great river in the island Atlantis') is among his best things: a divine indolence soaks it, and if there are better lines in English poetry there are none that breathe a more heartfelt peace than Ocean's:

> It is the unpastured sea hungering for calm:
> Peace, monster. I come now. Farewell.

The fourth act I shall not attempt to analyse. It is an intoxication, a riot, a complicated and uncontrollable splendour, long, and yet not too long, sustained on the note of ecstasy such as no other English poet, perhaps no other poet, has given us. It can be achieved by more than one artist in music: to do it in words has been, I think, beyond the reach of nearly all. It has not, and cannot have, the solemnity and overwhelming realism of the *Paradiso*, but it has all its fire and light. It has not the 'sober certainty of waking bliss' which makes Milton's paradise so inhabitable—but it sings from regions in our consciousness that Milton never entered.

Some anti-romantic repudiations of such poetry rest, perhaps, on a misunderstanding. It might be true, as the materialists must hold, that there is no possible way by which men can arrive at such felicity; or again, as Mr. Eliot and I believe, that there is one Way, and only one, and that Shelley has missed it. But while we discuss these things, the romantic poet has added meaning to the word Felicity itself. Whatever the result of our debate, we had better attend to his discovery lest we remain more ignorant than we need have been of the very thing about which we debated.

II

WILLIAM MORRIS

In ordinary life a thousand considerations prohibit for most
of us any complete working out of our responses: . . . but in
the 'imaginative experiences' these obstacles are removed.

I. A. RICHARDS, *Principles of Literary Criticism*, cap. **xxxi**

WILLIAM MORRIS

IT has been said that if you tell ten people you are reading Thomas Aquinas, nine will reply with something about angels dancing on the point of a needle. The saw is already out of date and Thomism in the ascendant; but it is worth remembering as a reminder of the misleading labels which great writers bear during the periods of their obscurity, and also of the sudden changes of fashion which strip those labels off. In spite of some excellent critics, William Morris is still commonly among the labelled. A mention of him in many literary circles still produces a torrent of objections which have been learned by heart—he wrote *Wardour Street*, he was a victim to false medievalism, his poetry is the poetry of escape, his stories are mere tapestries. It is true that these charges have never had any effect on his persistent admirers. But these are a company ill fitted to defend their favourite. They are few—though perhaps not so few as each in his solitude supposes—and they read humbly for the sake of pleasure, a pleasure so inexhaustible that after twenty or fifty years of reading they find it worked so deeply into all their emotions as to defy analysis. I knew one who could come no nearer to an explanation of Morris's charm than to repeat 'It's the Northernness—the Northernness'; and though I knew very well what he meant, I felt it was not war. Yet as the lovers of Morris now are, the lovers of Donne once were, and not so very long ago. It is possible that a critical revolution may yet embarrass these scattered and inoffensive readers with the discovery that what they regard as a private, perhaps a shamefaced, indulgence has all along been a gratifying proof of their penetration and 'contemporaneity.' The thing is feasible because even the sternest theories of literature cannot permanently suppress an author who is so obstinately pleasurable. It is certain that the common cries against Morris, where they are not mere ignorance, are based on *a priori* dogmatisms that will go down at a touch; and it is arguable that of all the romantics he lies least open to the usual attacks of what we may now,[1] perhaps, begin to call Georgian anti-romanticism.

The objection to his language is largely a hangover from the old Wordsworthian theory of diction. It is, of course, perfectly true that Morris invented for his poems and perfected in his prose-romances a language which has never at any period been spoken in England; but I suppose that most instructed people are now aware (as Wordsworth was not aware) that what we call 'ordinary' or 'straightforward' English prose, as we have all tried to write it since Dryden's time, is almost equally an artificial speech—a literary or 'hypothetical' language based on a French conception of elegance and a highly unphilological ideal of 'correctness'. When we begin to teach boys 'essay-writing' at school we are teaching them to translate into this language, and if they continue to write as they talk we plough them in School Certificate. The question about Morris's style is not whether it is an artificial language—all endurable language in longer works must be that—but whether

---

[1] Written in the reign of Edward VIII.

it is a good one. And it is here that sheer ignorance
begins to play its part. I cannot help suspecting that
most of the detractors when they talk of Morris's
style are really thinking of his printing: they expect
the florid and the crowded, and imagine something
like Sidney's *Arcadia*. In fact, however, this style
consistently departs from that of modern prose in the
direction of simplicity. Except for a few archaic
words—and since the appearance of the S.O.E.D. it is
a pleasure to be sent to the dictionary—it is incomparably easier and clearer than any 'natural' style
could possibly be, and the 'dull finish', the careful
avoidance of rhetoric, gloss, and decoration, is of its
very essence. Those who are really repelled by it
after a fair trial are being repelled not by its romanticism but by its classicism, for in one sense Morris is as
classical as Johnson. Long ago, Mr. Alfred Noyes
noticed the self-imposed limitation under which
Morris describes nature whether in prose or verse—
the birds that are merely 'brown', the sea that is
never anything more remarkable than 'blue' or
'green'. Morris, in fact, obeys the doctrine of generality; he does not number the streaks on the tulip but
'exhibits in his portraits of nature such prominent
and striking features as recall the original to every
mind'. That such 'just representations of general
nature' can, as Johnson claims, 'please many and
please long', his own writing, and that of Morris,
will equally prove.

'I sat down on a bank, such as a writer of romance
might have delighted to feign. I had indeed no trees to
whisper over my head, but a clear rivulet streamed at my

feet. The day was calm, the air was soft, and all was rude-
ness, silence and solitude.'

'The road was rough that day and they went not above
a foot pace the more part of the time; and daylong they
were going up and up, and it grew cold as the sun got low,
though it was yet summer.'

The first sentence is from Johnson and the second
from Morris. There are a dozen differences between
them, but there are two important similarities; both
are content with recording obvious facts in very
general language, and both succeed so that we really
taste the mountain air. It is, indeed, this matter-of-
factness, as Clutton-Brock pointed out, which lends
to all Morris's stories their sober air of conviction.
Other stories have only scenery: his have geography.
He is not concerned with 'painting' landscapes; he
tells you the lie of the land, and then you paint the
landscapes for yourself. To a reader long fed on the
almost botanical and entomological niceties of much
modern fiction—where, indeed, we mostly skip if the
characters go through a jungle—the effect is at first
very pale and cold, but also very fresh and spacious.
We begin to relish what my friend called the 'Northernness'. No mountains in literature are as far away
as distant mountains in Morris. The world of his
imagining is as windy, as tangible, as resonant and
three dimensional, as that of Scott or Homer.

He treats the passions, for the most part, in the
same way. A lover's night of anxiety for his mistress
who is a captive is thus described. 'He could not
choose but make stories of her meeting of the tyrant,
and her fear and grief and shame, and the despair of

her heart.' Morris does not particularize the imagery
that passed through the young man's mind; 'he could
not choose but make stories', that is all. Later in
the same book Morris has to describe the lover's
behaviour when alone with his mistress for some
weeks in the wilderness. It is a situation about which
almost any other author, sentimental, sensual, or
cynical, would have made what Locke calls a 'pud-
der'. Morris gives the fact—'All this while, he durst
not kiss or caress her save very measurely'—and the
reason 'for he deemed that she would not suffer it'.
What could be more sensible? And this brings us to
the whole question of Morris's treatment of love; it
is in this that he differs most remarkably from the
majority of romantics and is most immune from anti-
romantic criticism. On the one hand, it is no use
invoking modern psychology to reveal the concealed
eroticism in his imagination, because the eroticism
is not concealed: it is patent, ubiquitous, and un-
abashed. On the other hand, Morris, except in his
first volume and in such an anomalous poem as *Love
is Enough*, makes no attempt to paint Passion as
understood by the Romantics. Havelock Ellis's
definition of love ('lust *plus* friendship'), monstrously
inadequate if applied to the love expressed by Dante
or Coventry Patmore or Meredith, is a perfectly good
definition of love in Morris's stories—unless, indeed,
'lust' is too heavy and breathless a name for anything
so bright and youthful and functional as his kind of
sensuality. The experience of his lovers is at the
opposite extreme from the dizzying or swooning
states described in common romantic poetry. The

beauty of Keats's Madeline made Porphyro 'faint'.
But when the young man in the *Roots of the Mountains*
thought of the young woman's body 'it stirred him
up to go swiftlier as he strode on, the day brightening
behind him'. Morris, in fact, describes the sort of
love that is a function of health; it quickens a man's
pace. It is not surprising that the hero of the *Roots
of the Mountains* should soon after be in love with a
different woman. Morris does not deal much in
world-without-end fidelities, and his heroes are seldom so enamoured of one damsel that they are quite
indifferent to the beauty of others. When infidelities
occur they are, of course, regrettable, as any other
breach of faith, because they wound the social health
and harmony of the tribe; they are not felt as aposta-
sies from any god of love. Morris's Jason is felt to
be a treacherous and ungrateful man for deserting
Medea; but the poet does not share Chaucer's feeling
about the mere change of love considered in itself.
Still less does he understand the Christian and sacra-
mental view of such things. He is the most irreligious
of all our poets—*anima naturaliter pagana*.

To see this is, of course, to see that his medievalism
is a kind of accident. The real interests of the Middle
Ages—Christian mysticism, Aristotelian philosophy,
Courtly Love—mean nothing to him. The world of
the sagas, at once homely and heroic, is in some ways
more congenial to him than that of the romances,
just as their hard-bitten style with its almost excessive
use of litotes is of all influences upon his language the
most fruitful. That is another aspect of the 'Northernness'. But it would be a misunderstanding to inquire

into the date and place of the society he depicts:
you might as well apply historical criticism to Chaucer's Troy or Sidney's Arcadia or the plays of Lord
Dunsany. Morris chose to build up his imaginary
world on hints furnished by the Middle and the Dark
Ages as these existed in the imagination of his own time
and his own circle in particular. With that circle he
doubtless shared many historical errors. But his choice
was poetically right simply because that misconception of the Middle Ages (for reasons which go far back
into the time of Percy and the Wartons) already existed,
and existed poetically, in the public imagination. It
was, and to some extent still is, part of our mythology.

This is only to repeat that his stories in verse and
prose represent an imaginary world. It is a recognition of this fact which has earned them such epithets
as 'faint', 'shadowy', 'decorative', and the like. Nineteenth-century criticism was unconsciously dominated by the novel, and could praise only with
reservations work which does not present analysed
characters ('living men and women' as they called
them) in a naturalistic setting. Modern Shake-
spearian criticism dates from the abandonment of
the attempt to treat Shakespeare's plays as if they
were novels. The change perhaps began with
Raleigh's unemphasized observation that for Shakespeare plot comes first and character has to be fitted
into it. Since then such critics as Miss Spurgeon,
Stoll, and Wilson Knight have all, in their several
directions, moved away from the old conception.
We are free to recognize that in the *Winter's Tale* the
Pygmalion myth or resurrection myth in the last act

is the substance and the characters, motives, and half-hearted attempts at explanation which surround it are the shadow. We may even regret that the convention in which Shakespeare worked did not allow him to make Paulina frankly a fairy or an angel and thus be rid of his 'improbable possibilities'. It will soon, we may hope, be impossible to relegate Morris to the shades because his whole world is an invention. All we need demand is that this invented world should have some intellectual or emotional relevance to the world we live in.

And it has. The travels of the Argonauts or of those more ambitious wanderers in the *Earthly Paradise*, the quest for the well at the world's end or the wood beyond the world, the politics of Mirkwood and the sorrow of Odin the Goth—all these are attached in a dozen ways first to Morris's life and then to the lives of us all. They express the author's deepest sense of reality, which is much subtler and more sensitive than we expect—a mass of 'tensions' as von Hügel would have said. It is a pity that so many readers begin with the *Earthly Paradise*, not only because it contains much of his dullest work but also because it can hardly be understood in isolation. The opening stanzas state the theme of mutability and mortality, which seems at first a romantic commonplace, and the author seems himself to invite that very estimate of his work which I am rejecting, calling himself an idle singer, whose

> murmuring rhyme
> Beats with light wing against the ivory gate
> Telling a tale not too importunate.

It is only when we have read the Prologue and all the 'links' that we perceive this complaint of mortality as the recoil from a positive and violent passion for immortality. The Prologue, in fact, is the breaking of a wave: the whole of the rest of the book is 'the melancholy, long, withdrawing roar', and into it Morris has put all that negative and compensatory poetry which has earned him his reputation. The scheme could hardly have escaped monotony and he never tried it again. But even here the first 'tension' becomes visible and redeems the whole thing from mere *fin de siècle* pessimism. On the one hand we have the passion for immortality, which in Morris is as wild, as piercing, as orgiastic and heart-breaking as his presentations of sexual love are simple, sensuous, and unimpassioned; and this in itself is something very different from mere melancholy. But it is balanced by an opposite feeling which no one has expressed quite so forcibly as Morris—the feeling that such desire is not wholly innocent, that the world of mortality is more than enough for our allegiance, and that the traitor and apostate who follows a wilder possibility will look back too late on the

> land that might have been to me
> A kindly giver of wife, child, and friend
> And happy life, or at the worser end
> A quiet grave till doomsday rend the earth.

This poise between two moods must not be mistaken for a debate about two doctrines. Morris, like a true Pagan, does not tell us (because he does not think he knows) the ultimate significance of those moments in which we cannot help reaching out for something

beyond the visible world and so discovering 'at what
unmeasured price man sets his life'. He neither seeks
to justify them like a Christian nor to repress them
like a materialist. He simply presents the tension.
And it is one that cannot be resolved: for that same
impression of the goodness of mere living which cor-
rects our desire for some Acre of the Undying must
also aggravate the sting of mortality. As Byron had
said, there is no sterner moralist than pleasure; and
so for Morris it is not unhappiness but happiness
which is the real fountain of misgiving, making us
'more mindful that the sweet days die'. The idyllic,
which admittedly fills so large a place in his work, is
not simply an escape; its temporary exclusion of ill
luck, disease, and injustice serves to disengage the
real and unalterable trouble about temporal existence as such. It is as if Morris said to the ordinary
pessimists, 'Yes, yes, I know all about the slums, and
Tess, and Jude. Perhaps we can abolish them in a
rational society; but it is then that the real problem
appears.'

No doubt many will be tempted to reply that this
'is going far to seek disquietude' in a world where
scarce one per cent. of the population have ever been
so fortunate as to have leisure for those delicate dis-
tresses. But Morris has not left himself open to this
reply. No one could be less of 'a *cui bono* man'; no
one more concerned, both in practice and imagination, with 'the people's praise' and the 'good of the
folk'. This second tension, between the fundamental
unsatisfactoriness of mortal life and a conviction that
the vigorous enjoyment and improvement of such

life is infinitely worth while, now begins to appear.
Already in *The Life and Death of Jason* the haunting
desire for immortality is opposed—and, again, I do
not mean *doctrinally* opposed—not so much to ordinary happiness as to heroic exploit. The Argonauts
are teased and solicited over and over again by
paradises, gardens, and islands, 'not made for men
that die', and every pause of the action is but a
silence to make audible the

> Formless and wailing thoughts that press
> About our hour of happiness.

But the answer to these is simply to get on with the
job—to mend the sails, or launch the boat, or gather
firewood. This admirable solution—at times almost
as surprising as that in the *Bhagavad-Gita*, 'Defeat and
victory are the same: therefore fight'—becomes more
and more characteristic of Morris as he proceeds. In
Sigurd it amounts almost to a complete trampling
underfoot of the whole ideal of happiness in any
shape or form. It is contemptible to ask 'a little
longer and a little longer to live'. The gods have not
made the world for happiness but to be 'a tale', and
it is good, when they ask us for one deed, to give them
two. We find even a hint that there may be some
ultimate justification of all things which will explain

Why the brave man's spear is broken and his war-shield
    fails at need.

But Morris soon withdraws from these supposals.
For one so enamoured of 'the Northernness' these
doomed Eddaic gods—the very type of Stoical Romanticism—had a strong appeal. But Morris cannot

forget that he does not really know whether anything like them exists, and he feels that the whole thing is getting too like a philosophy or a theology. He will not hammer his world into any simplified shape. Hence in the great prose romances, which are the real crown of his work, we come back to something much more actual. The answer to the 'formless and wailing thoughts' is found in the daily life, health, and preservation of the community. The 'kindreds', 'houses', or 'little lands' of the romances are the points where Morris's career as a socialist touches his career as a poet. For Morris—let there be no mistake about it—is in one sense as good a 'totalitarian' as ever came out of Moscow or Berlin; his romantic socialism, if it be romantic, is at the opposite pole from the individualism of Shelley or Tom Payne. He immerses the individual completely in the society. 'If thou diest today, where then shall our love be?' asks the heroine in the *House of the Wolfings*. 'It shall abide with the soul of the Wolfings', comes the answer. The good tribesman cannot 'see' the 'grave-night', but rather the 'tale of the Wolfings through the coming days' and himself 'amidst it ever reborn and yet reborn'. The opposite state of mind is an enchantment of the dwarfs, when a man becomes separated in soul from the kindred—'I loved them not and was not of them, and outside myself there was nothing: *within me was the world.*' The last words, which I have ventured to italicize, are Morris's penetrating analysis of the poison inherent in one type of romanticism: its *dandyism*, and subjectivity, and its pitiful war-cry *au moins je suis autre*. Morris

has nothing here to learn from our own century.
Rather he has something to teach. Many sociological
writers are dull because while they talk of a just
distribution of goods they give us no assurance that
they know what Good means: we remain in doubt
lest the gold they would distribute so equitably may
be but fairy gold which will turn by daylight into
ballot papers or soup tickets. The great use of the
idyllic in literature is to find and illustrate the good
—to give a real value to the *x* about which political
algebra can then work. The tribal communities
which Morris paints in *The House of the Wolfings* or
The Roots of the Mountains are such attempts, perhaps
the most successful attempts ever made, to give *x* a
value. Morris knows as concretely as Burke or Tolstoy
what he wants. A modern poet of the Left, praising
that same solidarity with the group which Morris
praises, invites a man to be 'one cog in the singing
golden hive'. Morris, on the other hand, paints the
actual going on of the communal life, the sowing,
planting, begetting, building, ditching, eating, and
conversation. And for this reason, where the modern
poet (squeezing two of the commonest journalistic
metaphors together, whether inadvertently or in the
vain hope of a lively oxymoron) goes no deeper than
the excitement of a political meeting, Morris, from
remote Mirkwood and unhistoric Burgstead, brings
back a sentiment that a man could really live by. He
may seem, in one way, to be as ideal as Shelley, but
in another he is as earthy, as rooted, as Aristotle or
Dr. Johnson. He is everywhere concrete. Comte's
'subjective immortality' and Godwin's 'benevolence'

E

are mere philosophemes: Morris's life beyond life
with the soul of the Wolfings, because we know them
and indeed are bone of their bone, is something solid.
He tells of what he has tried and found good.

I spoke just now of the enchantment which separated one of Morris's heroes from this unity. Significantly, it came from a 'dwarf-wrought hauberk'
which offered him immunity from death. His
temptation to use it and his final rejection of it are
the main theme of *The House of the Wolfings*: the
conflict between the love of the tribe and the fear of
death is here explicit. And if Morris were mainly
concerned with the fear of death, this romance would
have resolved the tension, for on this level life and
death with the kindred has only to be seen to be
preferred to anything else in the world or out of the
world. But the fear of death was never one of Morris's
chief concerns: it is only an aspect of something very
different, and much harder to extinguish—the positive and passionate thirst for immortality. And so
the solution is only momentary: in the romances that
follow, the rebel passion breaks out again, never more
impressive than when it is thus expressed by an old,
unwearied poet. In the later romances the claims of
the tribe are not forgotten, and the young hero who
goes to the end of the world to drink of the well of
life carries thither with him, and carries back, the
determination to settle down and be a good king in
his own small country. No wanderings are allowed
to obliterate our love for 'the little platoon we belong
to'. The tension is felt not now between the love
of mortal life and the longing for immortality; it is

rather discovered within the longing itself. We cannot help wishing that human life and youth should
last for ever: yet is it really to be wished? Long ago in
Jason Morris had hinted that life owes all its sweets
to that same death whence rise all its bitters. He had
stumbled unawares on the real dialectic of natural
desire which cannot help wanting (as philosophers
would say) 'the bad infinite', though that infinite is
a horror and a torment. In *The Story of the Glittering
Plain* the land of the ever-living is reached, but it
turns out to be only a gorgeous prison. The hero
finds 'the falseness of this unchanging land': among
its 'soft and merry folk' he 'longs for the house of his
fathers and the men of the spear and the plough'.
So in *The Well at the World's End* the Innocent folk,
whose name is significant, say that 'the gods have
given us the gift of death lest we weary of life'.

If we were dealing with any author but Morris
we should say that this is the conclusion of the whole
matter. But in Morris there are no conclusions. The
opposed desires change into their opposites and are
lulled asleep and reawake; balance is attained and
immediately lost; everything is always beginning
over again: it is a dance, not a diagram. It can no
more be seized in an epigram, summed up and
docketed, than experience itself. One feeling alone
never alters, and attains something of the stability of
a doctrine. He is always sure that we must labour
for the kindred and 'love the earth and the world
with all our souls'. This is the central altar: the
dance moves round it. Love of the world and earth
must tempt desire to sail beyond the frontier of that

earth and world. Those who sail must look back
from shoreless seas to find that they have abandoned
their sole happiness. Those who return must find
that happiness once more embittered by its mortality,
must long again. Even if we found what we wanted
it might be the ruin, not the consummation, of desire.
But we cannot therefore cease to desire it. This hither-
ing and thithering is too irregular and shot too full of
colours to be compared to the sad Buddhist wheel, the
circle too beautiful to be called a vicious circle; the
conclusion drawn, wherever a mere luxury of pessimism threatens, is always practical, heroic, and com-
monsensible. And as the world of Morris cannot
be summed up, so Morris himself escapes definition.
What shall we call him? An imaginative Positivist
—an animal man flawed by the longing for a
coloured cloud—a potential mystic inhibited by a
too-convinced love of the material world—all these
err by representing as fixed something which is
really always in solution. It is better to say simply
that he is a good story-teller who has presented
perhaps more faithfully than any other writer the
whole scene of life as it must appear on the natural
level.

The old indeterminate, half-Christian, half-Pan-
theistic, piety of the last century is gone. The modern
literary world is increasingly divided into two camps,
that of the positive and militant Christians and that
of the convinced materialists. It is here that Morris
may be of incalculable value in saving us from 'dis-
sociation'; for both camps can find in him something
that they need. The appeal of this Pagan poet to the

Christian reader is obvious. No one else states quite
so clearly that dilemma in the natural virtues and the
natural desires from which all philosophical religion
must start—the question which all theologies claim
to answer. And Morris is the more precious because
he is content simply to state the question. His work
is the fresh fruit of naïve experience, uncontaminated
by theorizing. When William Allingham in 1882
talked to him 'among other things of believing or not
believing in a God' he replied, 'It's so unimportant'
and 'went on to say that all we can get to, do what
we will, is a form of words'. This scepticism—a true
scepticism with no unacknowledged bias to the negative—leaves his statement of Pagan experience chemi-
cally pure. If he had started from the concept of
Eternity we might suspect his exposure of the dialectic of time to be tendentious: as it is, the exposure
is forced upon him by mere obedience to desire and
he remains quite unaware of the doctrines which
he is supporting. He thus becomes one of the greatest Pagan witnesses—a prophet as unconscious, and
therefore as far beyond suspicion, as Balaam's ass.
As for the readers of the Left, I do not say that they
will find him directly useful in politics. His conception of public good is too deeply rooted in agriculture,
handicrafts, and the family to be applied to any
modern Utopia. What will interest the Left will
be those very same qualities that interest the Christians. The Left agrees with Morris that it is an absolute duty to labour for human happiness in this
world. But the Left is deceiving itself if it thinks that
any zeal for this object can permanently silence the

reflection that every moment of this happiness must be lost as soon as gained, that all who enjoy it will die, that the race and the planet themselves must one day follow the individual into a state of being which has no significance—a universe of inorganic homogeneous matter moving at uniform speed in a low temperature. Hitherto the Left has been content, as far as I know, to pretend that this does not matter. It has perhaps been afraid of the 'formless and wailing thoughts' because these seem to lead inevitably into the paralysing kind of pessimism—'there be some that say, who shall shew us any good?' At the same time, modern psychology does not encourage us to base a single life, much less a civilization, on so gigantic a repression. It is here, surely, that Morris can come to their assistance. In Morris they will find a political creed which is, in principle, the same as their own, combined with an absolute refusal to paint out 'the great bar of black that runs across the shield of man.' Morris will show them how to acknowledge what they are tempted to camouflage and yet not to draw from it the conclusion they rightly fear. Nay, he will show them how this thirst for immortality, tinglingly alive in the perpetual motion of its dialectic, will but add a more urgent motive to their endeavours, an honourable firmness in defeat, and a keener edge to victory.

For Morris has 'faced the facts'. This is the paradox of him. He seems to retire far from the real world and to build a world out of his wishes; but when he has finished the result stands out as a picture of experience ineluctably true. No full-grown mind wants optimism or pessimism—philosophies of the nursery where they are not philosophies of the clinic; but to have presented in one vision the ravishing sweetness and the heart-breaking melancholy of our experience, to have shown how the one continually passes over into the other, and to have combined all this with a stirring practical creed, this is to have presented the *datum* which all our adventures, worldly and other-worldly alike, must take into account. There are many writers greater than Morris. You can go on from him to all sorts of subtleties, delicacies, and sublimities which he lacks. But you can hardly go behind him.

III

THE IDEA OF AN 'ENGLISH SCHOOL'

Non leve quiddam interest inter humanae mentis idola et divinae mentis ideas, hoc est inter placita quaedam inania et veras signaturas atque impressiones factas in creaturis, prout inveniuntur.

BACON, *Novum Organum*, i. 23

Read to a joint meeting of the Classical and English Associations

THE IDEA OF AN 'ENGLISH SCHOOL'

THE title of this paper is unfortunate in recalling that of Newman's best book. It is doubly unfortunate in so far as it not only suggests, on my part, an arrogant intention of pitting myself against so great a writer, but also carries with it an omen of failure on the practical side; for none of the things which Newman advised has come to pass. Yet some such title is unavoidable. I intend, it is true, to talk a good deal about the Final Honour School of English as it actually exists at Oxford. But I am concerned with that School not as an historical fact but as an approximation to an ideal. What we are doing at Oxford is of universal interest only as an indication of what, on my view, we are trying to do or ought to do. We are doubtless full of faults and do not shun criticism, provided such criticism is based on an understanding of our aims. You may not agree with these aims— though I hope that you will—but do not blame a man for making slow progress to the North when he is trying to get to the East.

We are under no illusions as to our reputation in the outer world. What our enemies think of us is vigorously enough, if not always very lucidly, conveyed by the expressions they use—by their references to 'the Germanic jungle', 'all this philology', 'Verner's law', 'Anglo-Saxon', and (most damning of all) 'Gothic'. When we listen attentively to this buzz of condemnation, we think that we can distinguish two strains in it. The confusion between 'Germanic' or 'Anglo-Saxon' on the one hand and 'philology' or

'Verner's law' on the other, is made, we believe, by two classes of people. In the first class we find the man who is still living in the Renaissance, the belated Ascham, who is quite sure that literature he cannot translate must be bad literature—must be 'Gothic' in the classical sense of the word. He does not like the poetry of the Dark, and Middle Ages (*ignoti nulla cupido*) and he uses 'philology' simply as a term of abuse. He is not really thinking of philology at all. In the second class we find a much more respectable opponent, probably a real scholar who knows that he does not know any medieval language. His objection is not to the unknown literatures—in such a man it could not be—but to comparative philology. He has in his mind the picture of a promising academic discipline, in which the young might have been guided to a systematic study of our English classics, not without some subsidiary Greek and Latin to steady their judgement, perverted and thwarted by irrelevant excursions into Germanic philology; he sees the interest which ought to have been concentrated on Shakespeare and Johnson dissipated on mere comparisons between English and cognate languages; and he wonders why English should have been selected to carry this purely scientific and un-literary burden which might, with equal propriety or impropriety, have been bound on the back of several other subjects.

To this second, and reasonable, type of critic, our reply is a simple one. His information is out of date. No undergraduate at Oxford is obliged to know a single word of Gothic, old High German, or Old

Norse, or to study the relations between these languages and his own. The English student can choose between three alternative courses, all of which can conduct him to the highest honours. One of these is frankly medieval, and if a student chooses it he does so because he is interested in early English and its immediate relatives. The second is a half-way house —a complicated affair that need not now concern us. The third is the literary course proper, which the vast majority of our students take.

But here comes the rub. This third and literary course, I must confess, contains three papers which the enemy will be tempted to describe as 'philological'. The first is on Modern English, and deals mainly with the history of meaning, whether in syntax or vocabulary. The second is on Anglo-Saxon texts, and the third on Middle English texts. I do not imagine that the critic I have in view will object very strongly to the first of these. If he does, the official voice of our English School will reply with the very pertinent question, 'Do you wish students to understand what they read or not?' For the fact is that those who have had no experience in the teaching of English are living in a fool's paradise as regards the ability of the average undergraduate to *construe* his mother tongue. Again and again curious statements in the essays of our pupils can be traced back to an original failure to make out the sense of Milton or Johnson or Coleridge, as a schoolboy fails to make out the sense of Caesar or Xenophon. And with this answer I expect that the critics will be satisfied. But the other two papers—the Anglo-Saxon and Middle

English texts—I fear he will regard as *vestigial*, as relics of that philological period in which, admittedly, English studies at Oxford began—*ein Theil des Theils, der anfangs alles war*. He will be in danger of looking upon them as a rearguard which has not yet been defeated but whose defeat may be hourly expected. His hopes are vain; and it is at this point that I must join issue with him. If any of the three papers is really vestigial, it is the paper on Modern English. I have just stated the official defence for it; but it would be disingenuous not to confess that this paper is a subject of dispute among ourselves. I am, in fact, one of those who disapprove of it. But that is not our present concern. I mention it only to emphasize the fact that this paper is incomparably the most philological of the three, and that the other two, so far from being vestigial, are essential to the idea of an English school as I see it.

Before I attempt to explain why, I must remove two possible misconceptions. One is the belief that Anglo-Saxon is a language other than English, or even, as used to be said, that English is a third language born from the union of two earlier languages, Anglo-Saxon and French. This is an error so gross that six weeks' study would remove it from the minds of the most prejudiced. You might as well say that Latin was a new language born from the union of Roman and Greek. Anglo-Saxon is simply early English. Norman-French is simply one of the foreign languages which, from time to time, have enriched our vocabulary. Most of the changes which separate what we call Anglo-Saxon from what we call Middle

English had begun before the Normans landed, and would have followed much the same course if no Conquest had ever occurred. Brevity compels me to be dogmatic; but it is not really a subject that admits of discussion.

The second misconception turns on our old friend 'philology'. There is no philology in the papers on Anglo-Saxon and Middle English. They are papers on texts, consisting of a core of passages for translation surrounded by questions on archaeological, textual, cultural, or historical matters relevant to the texts. The student is asked to know about *Beowulf* or *Pearl* just those things which the classical examiner demands that he should know about Virgil or Sophocles. Philology is absent, unless you call grammar philology. Before some audiences I should feel it my duty to insist rather strongly on the value of grammar. I am told that there have been critics of Chaucer who perpetrated serious blunders in translation, and built up formidable aesthetic superstructures on a purely intuitive, and sometimes erroneous, conception of their author's meaning. But I presume that every one present agrees that if you are going to read a book at all, it is desirable to be able to tell which words are in the Nominative and which are in the Accusative.

We are now, at last, in a position to come to grips with the main question. Granted that these old books are written in what is unmistakably English, and granted that we do not set philological questions on them, still, it will be asked, why should we read them? What relevance has the study of *Beowulf* for the man who wants to read modern English literature? If we are looking for sheer poetical merit, are there not many poems greater than *Beowulf* and no more difficult? Why not the *Iliad*, or the *Aeneid*? If, on the other hand, we are looking for the origins of Modern literature, shall we not find them in Rome and Greece? None of our great poets could read Anglo-Saxon: nearly all of them could and did read Latin, and some knew Greek.

I will take the second question first, and before I attempt to answer it, let me protest that I am no enemy of the classics. I have read the *Aeneid* through more often than I have read any long poem; I have just finished re-reading the *Iliad*; to lose what I owe to Plato and Aristotle would be like the amputation of a limb. Hardly any lawful price would seem to me too high for what I have gained by being made to learn Latin and Greek. If any question of the value of classical studies were before us, you would find me on the extreme right. I do not know where the last ditch in our educational war may be at the moment; but point it out to me on the trench-map and I will go to it. At present, however, we are only asking whether it is true that the origins of English literature are to be found in the classics. And perhaps if 'the origins' here means 'all the origins' no one, however, ignorant, would answer Yes. At most our critics can only mean that of the innumerable debts which our literary tradition owes, the debt to Rome and Greece is the greatest and most important. I do not think this is true.

The first step in an inquiry into its truth is to rule out the greatest Greek poets and philosophers.

Except on a few isolated writers such as Milton and
Gray, these have no influence worth talking about
before the nineteenth century. Chapman's Homer,
and even Pope's, might almost have been written to
prove that Homer was invisible to Englishmen until
the Romantic Revival had cleared their eyes. In
drama, Seneca is of far more importance than all the
Greek tragedians put together. The real Plato
counts for less in our tradition than that strange
theosophy which Ficino and others called 'Platonic
theology'. Aristotle, I admit, in a slightly Thomized
form, bit deeply into the mind of the Middle Ages;
but where are the literary results of this? On seven-
teenth-century criticism we can trace his influence at
every step, but it is an influence almost wholly mis-
chievous.

Having got rid of these august but irrelevant
names, it will be well to remind ourselves of the
authors who have really affected us deeply and over
long periods. Of the Romans those naturally come
first who enjoyed the same degree and nearly the
same kind of prestige both before and after the
Renaissance—the great Kings whose reign had begun
before *Beowulf* was written and has not ended yet.
I mean, of course Boethius, Ovid, and Virgil—and I
would put them roughly in that order of importance.
Immediately below these, in length and security of
reign, we might put Juvenal, the moral works of
Cicero and Seneca, Horace, Statius, Claudian, and a
few others. Apuleius and the elder Pliny would come
a good deal higher than they do in our modern scho-
lastic tradition. Of the Greeks, the great gossiping

F

authors, the repositories of anecdote, like Plutarch
and Diogenes Laertius, would stand at the top of the
list. Second to these we should find, indistinguish-
ably blended, the joint influence of Theocritus and
the novelists—Longus, Heliodorus, and the like; and
perhaps—but I am doubtful about my facts here—
the influence of the Anthology.

Having identified the influential authors it remains
to consider what their influence really was. It is clear,
in the first place, that our literature is not greatly
indebted to them for its forms. We are apt to forget
that Milton's classical epic and classical tragedy are
lonely exceptions. Most attempts to transplant an
ancient form into English literature have failed.
Milton is the single survivor in a forlorn hope where
Cowley, Blackmore, and Glover fell: *Samson* lives,
but *Gorboduc*, *Cato*, and *Caractacus* do not. A list of our
best narrative poems would contain *Troilus*, *The
Faerie Queene*, *the Prelude*, *Don Juan*, and *Endymion*, and
would leave out all our classical epics save one. A list
of our greatest dramas would give an even more
striking result. Our lyric poetry is, no doubt, richly
decorated in certain periods with borrowings from
ancient Latin and Greek, though they are not more
numerous than its borrowings from medieval Latin,
from Italian, and from old and modern French. Its
chief serious attempt to adopt an ancient form, however, has left behind it only one or two successes by
Gray amidst a ruinous waste of 'Pindarique Odes';
and in the very nature of things formal similarities
between quantitative lyric and rhymed accentual
lyric must be very superficial. Already in *Summer is*

icumen in we are basing our lyrical poetry on discoveries in music which the Greeks never made.
The novel, born from the marriage of the periodical
essay and the romance, or the sonnet, descending
from the Provençals, are even farther removed from
ancient literature. The Satire and the Pastoral are
more instructive, for in them we can see side by side
the unhappy attempts to adhere to the classical form
and the happy departures from it. The Roman
model—the static, rambling diatribe—is preserved
by Donne, Hall, Marston, and Churchill, and by
Pope in his inferior works; our great satires, deserting
this in favour of extravagant satiric fiction and owing
something, perhaps, to Lucian and the *Margites*, but
much more to Rabelais and Cervantes, have given
us *Hudibras, Absalom, The Rape, The Dunciad, Gulliver,
Don Juan, Erewhon,* and *Brave New World.* In the
Pastoral we can trace both developments in the same
writer (and that, not only in English) as we gratefully
lay aside Sannazaro's tedious *Piscatory Eclogues* and
open his *Arcadia* or turn from the fussy futility of the
Shepherds Calendar to the sixth book of *The Faerie
Queene.* The little drop of Theocritus properly mixed
with northern romance and Provençal love poetry
improves the drink: offer it neat, and our stomachs
turn. We can read Sidney and William Browne, but
who, unbribed, would open the pastorals of Mantuan,
Barclay, or Googe?

But perhaps I have argued too long on a point that
is obvious. No one can really be maintaining that the
best and most characteristic English work is deeply
indebted to the classics for its form. We are more

likely to be told that something subtler than a form—
a spirit or temper or attitude—has been transferred.
And, of course, I have no wish to deny that many
individual English authors have in this way been
deeply affected by their classical reading. We cannot
even imagine Chapman without the Stoics, Burke
without Cicero, or Tennyson without Virgil. It is
equally true, however, that we cannot imagine
Chaucer without Guillaume de Lorris, or Spenser
without Ariosto, or Morris without Froissart and the
Edda. Of tracing such individual affinities there
would be no end. What the argument requires is to
show that the spirit of our literature, or our best literature, or most of our best literature, is closer to that
of the classics than to that of other cultures. And this,
I think, has never been shown.

Ovid's erotic poetry, received by our culture, becomes the poetry of Courtly Love; his mythological
poetry becomes the wonder tales of Chaucer and
Gower, the allegorical and astrological pantheon of
Fulgentius and Lydgate, the gods of Botticelli, Titian,
and Tintoretto, the emblematic deities of masque and
ballet and pantomime, and the capitalized abstractions of eighteenth-century verse. The tale of Troy
wears casque and habergeon in the fourteenth, lace
and periwig in the eighteenth, century. The Pastoral,
snatched from those realistic Sicilian slopes, is carried
into the depths of an Arcadian golden age and there
enchanted. The change which the classics undergo
when we take them into our own imagination is precisely a change of spirit or temper. Names and myths
remain, but all is romanticized, darkened here and

softened there, filled with new shadows and assimi-
lated to our needs. There is no question of new wine
being poured into old bottles: rather, a little new
wine is poured into a lot of old wine. We were not an
emptiness which the classics filled, nor a patient on
which they acted. We had our own idiosyncrasy.
We also were a spirit, an ancient, complex, and
intensely active spirit. We let in what we could turn
to our own substance, and the process of digestion
was thorough. *Quidquid recipitur, recipitur ad modum
recipientis.* Of this *recipiens*, the real English Muse, the
mother of us all, I shall have more to say in a few
moments. She is, you will notice, the person who has
hitherto been left out of the story.

My present duty, however, is to answer the question I set myself: what did the influence of the classics
really amount to? And already, I fear, it may seem
to you that I have proved too much. If they gave us
neither form nor spirit, then what, in heaven's name,
is this debt to them which even I acknowledge? The
answer to that is a very simple one. They gave us
Matter: not a new way of writing and feeling, but
new things to write and feel about—theories, his-
tories, facts, myths, anecdotes, people. That is why
the gossiping or encyclopaedic authors, like Plutarch,
Pliny, Diogenes Laertius, Aulus Gellius, and Macro-
bius, are so important. This is the real impress which
classical education has left on our literature. You
can read English poetry for days on end without
coming across classic form or classic feeling; but you
will have been inundated with references to how
Acteon died or what birds saved the Capitol, what

Agesilaus said or Pompey did, the constitution of Sparta, the matrimonial troubles of Socrates, and some one's witty reply to Alexander. It is this kind of influence that lies on the surface of our literature and meets every one's gaze; and it is of this that most people are really thinking when they say that our origins are in Greece and Rome.

But a source of matter is a very different thing from a source of inspiration, a real influence on form and spirit. The difference becomes clear if we compare the effect of the Classics upon us with the effect of a force that reached us a few centuries before the Renaissance. I promised, a minute ago, to say something more of our mother, the English Muse—the *recipiens* who receives everything in her own fashion. It is now time to remind you that long before this mother of ours met with Greek literature, she had already had a lover—a much more masterful lover whom she has never yet been able to forget. I mean, of course, Old French. I have said that you can read English poetry for a long time without coming across classic form. You cannot read one verse, unless it is *vers libre*, without meeting Old French form. It was Old French that overthrew our native prosody: we have been singing an old French tune ever since. It was Old French that taught us those species of sentiment and refinement which we still use. Whenever you think of a rhyme for a limerick, or accept fictitious prose narrative as an obvious form of serious literature, or offer a chair to a lady, or build a castle instead of a villa in the air, you are being Old French. You can choose, to some extent, how classical you will be; you cannot choose how Old French you will be. The thing is in our system, bred in the bone. This is a real influence. Compared with it the influence of the classics is recent, superficial, almost negligible.

You will have noticed that this casts a disquieting light on our educational problem. If we are to seek the true sources of our own literature, then the serious rival to Anglo-Saxon is not the classics, but Old French. If we abandon *Beowulf* we must put in not Homer but the *Romance of the Rose*, and that for two reasons. In the first place, as I have said, the old French influence is incomparably greater in degree. But secondly, it is of a kind that cannot be studied at second hand. A real transfusion of spirit involves intangibles: to study it is to study things that can only be known by long and sympathetic reading of originals. But the matter, which is what we have mainly borrowed from Greece and Rome can be quite adequately learned from Classical Dictionaries, historical text-books, and translations. Do not misunderstand the word 'adequately'. I do not mean that we shall thus have an adequate knowledge of the classics, but that we shall have an adequate preparation for the study of English. We shall have learned what our authors learned and often in the same way. A great deal of the classical ornament in English poetry was learned from text-books like Natalis Comes and Lemprière, and from translations like North's *Plutarch*. Pope found that he could very comfortably make a version of Homer without seriously learning Greek.

The real choice, then, is between Anglo-Saxon and Old French (or, perhaps, medieval Latin[1]), and if I choose the former it is again in virtue of the principle *Quidquid recipitur*. Our mother surrendered more to Old French than to the classics, but she did not surrender completely: even in the eleventh century she had a spirit of her own capable of transforming and assimilating what she received, modifying its gallantries with a homelier affection, hardening its heroisms, neglecting its ironies, broadening its humour, deepening its pathos, shading its marvels with a more awe-inspiring obscurity, and accentualizing its syllabic verse. And so, in the end, I am driven back to our ancient alliterative poetry. There for the first time I find a prosody based on the same speech rhythms that I hear in conversation to-day. I find a sense of language so native to us all that the phrases which hit the eighth-century audience hard, hit me hard too as soon as I have learned to understand them; I see at once that words like *gold* and *wolf* and *heart* and *blood* and *winter* and *earth*, had the same overtones for them as for me. Everything is already unmistakably English. This mere Englishness is usually called Romanticism by those who do not know Anglo-Saxon. They are fond of tracing it to the French Revolution or even to the Celtic strain in our blood. They bring far-fetched explanations why the English wrote melancholy poems about ruins in the eighteenth century, not knowing that the English had

---

[1] On further consideration I should regard the claims of medieval Latin as almost equal to those of Old French. It would not, at present, be easy to put the relevant texts in the hands of students, and they are hard to translate.

begun to do so in the eighth. When they read of remote wanderings upon strange seas in Morris or Coleridge they think the emotion in which such things are steeped by these poets essentially modern, and contrast it with the unambiguous simplicity of the *Odyssey* where the wanderer desires nothing but to get home. The contrast is just; but the English mood is not modern. The same thing is to be found in Anglo-Saxon poetry, associated, too, as Wordsworth might associate it, with the call of the cuckoo. Indeed the *Odyssey* is everywhere instructive as a contrast to our oldest poetry; Grendel and the Cyclops,[1] at the very beginning of the two literatures, symbolize their difference—the one so dark, so mysterious, so fitted to be the central symbol of evil in a great poem; the other so matter of fact, so accidental, so blasphemously tracing his descent from a god though he is the enemy of man. Virgil, as in space, so in temper, is the middle point between Homer and *Beowulf*, holding out his left hand to the colour and clarity of the Greek, his right to our English poet whom he so resembles in melancholy without pessimism, in half-articulate piety, and, above all, in his sense of the past. I doubt if Homer would really have appreciated *horrendum silvis et religione parentum* or the whole conception of Latium as Lurkwood (*quia his latuisset in oris*) as any Englishman of any period must do.

If, then, we are concerned with origins, Anglo-Saxon must keep its place in any English syllabus—

---

[1] See, on this point, J. R. R. Tolkien's indispensable *Beowulf: the Monsters and the Critics*.

nor is it improper, at this stage, to add that the majority of the students like it. In the old philological days they did not; now they do. But, of course, continuity is not everything, and we have not yet considered the man who says: 'The origins of English literature may be as you say. All I know is I had rather my boy read Homer than *Beowulf*.' This is a very legitimate preference, and of course the most natural way of gratifying it is to persuade the young man to take up classics instead of English. We are to suppose, however, that this is for some reason impossible: what the father wants is not classics instead of English but classics somehow included in English.

I would like to pass over all the practical difficulties of such a proposal, great as they are, because the question of principle involved goes right down to the roots of a man's educational theory. The English School as it stands has chosen unity and continuity: that is to say, taking a given area of reality, it has chosen, so far as possible, to explore it thoroughly, following the natural structure of that area, and neglecting all the interesting and delightful things over the frontier. The alternative school which is suggested, with Greek, Latin, and perhaps French classics side by side with the greatest English writers would be based on a different principle—the principle of selection. In the one you turn the young out into a single, untidy country to make what they can of it; in the other you take them to what their elders think the five or six most interesting places in a whole continent. It is the difference between knowing, say, Worcestershire inside out, while remaining ignorant

of the rest of the world, and knowing four or five
European capitals while striking no roots in any
single European soil. The choice is a very difficult
one. On the one hand we have Arnold's ideal—'the
best that is known and thought in the world'; on the
other *Spartam nactus es*. Embrace the latter and you
may become insular and provincial; embrace the
former and you may be a mere tourist, glib in all
countries and rooted in none. Which is the more
deeply ignorant, the shepherd who has never left the
Cotswolds, or the Peripatetic millionaire—the tap-
room of the 'Red Lion', or the lounge of the Palace
Hotel?

Where a final choice is so difficult I would recom-
mend a compromise. I think that the high lights
chosen by his elders and the wide area of ordinary
country explored on his own, are both necessary
elements in a man's education. But I feel very
strongly that the place for the selected high lights is
the school, and the place for the other is the University. It is natural and necessary that we should begin
by giving a boy the keys to some four or five chambers
of knowledge which we think the best, but it is equally
natural to let a man choose which he will to live in.
The true nature of this change is obscured if we say
that we believe in 'increasing specialization': for
specialization suggests narrowing and narrowing
suggests confinement. Now there is, of course, an
obvious sense in which the specialist is narrower than
the man reading a selection of 'great literatures'.
But is there not a sense in which he is freer? Any
balanced course of English and Classics which we

could draw up would bear the imprint of cultural ideals peculiar to an age and a class much more un-mistakably than a school of mere English need do. 'English', including Anglo-Saxon and Middle English along with modern English, including what we ordinarily call the 'dull' periods as well as the 'great' ones, is an object more or less presented to us by nature: the balanced course would be *our* selection, a selection which, in obedience to our local and momentary ideals, would cut across the joints, or veins, or grain of reality. The one is given, the other a construction. And it must be our construction, not the student's. We are doing for him one of the things he ought to do for himself. Our wild, rough English course has already thrown up interesting discoveries: the dull and difficult periods which any one working on the selective principle twenty years ago would have omitted to make room for foreign dainties, are turning out not to be dull at all, and Anglo-Saxon technical influences have appeared in the work of our younger poets. In other words, having kept our eye on the object and not on our own preconceptions, we are learning; we know more than we did. But this would have been quite impossible if we had begun with a syncretism of the 'best' in two or three different literatures. 'The best' could only have meant what a committee of four or five dons, brought up in a particular tradition, happened to think the best. We should have been dictating the course of future knowledge and taste on the authority of our existing taste and ignorance. A discipline so formed would be incapable of growth. No more would come out of it than had been put into it; and real advance in our knowledge of English would be made, if at all, by real scholars working privately in country rectories and London lodging-houses in contemptuous independence of us.

Such is my idea of an English school, and that is why the classics find no place in it. Need I say that I should like English students to know Greek and Latin? But they must not come to an English school to learn them. If they have not learned them before they come to me, I should like them to learn them after they leave me. Any proposal which enables them to do so in those postgraduate years which are increasingly spent at the university will always have all the support I can give it; and to that end I am ready to sacrifice any amount of what is called 'Research'.

IV

OUR ENGLISH SYLLABUS

'I do not like her name.'
'There was no thought of pleasing you when
she was christened.'

SHAKESPEARE

Read to the English Society at Oxford

OUR ENGLISH SYLLABUS

SCHOOLMASTERS in our time are fighting hard in defence of education against vocational training; universities, on the other hand, are fighting against education on behalf of learning.

Let me explain. The purpose of education has been described by Milton as that of fitting a man 'to perform justly, skilfully, and magnanimously all the offices both private and public, of peace and war'. Provided we do not overstress 'skilfully' Aristotle would substantially agree with this, but would add the conception that it should also be a preparation for leisure, which according to him is the end of all human activity. 'We wage war in order to have peace; we work in order to have leisure.' Neither of them would dispute that the purpose of education is to produce the good man and the good citizen, though it must be remembered that we are not here using the word 'good' in any narrowly ethical sense. The 'good man' here means the man of good taste and good feeling, the interesting and interested man, and almost the happy man. With such an end in view education in most civilized communities has taken much the same path; it has taught civil behaviour by direct and indirect discipline, has awakened the logical faculty by mathematics or dialectic, and has endeavoured to produce right sentiments— which are to the passions what right habits are to the body—by steeping the pupil in the literature both sacred and profane on which the culture of the community is based. Vocational training, on the other hand, prepares the pupil not for leisure, but for work; it aims at making not a good man but a good banker, a good electrician, a good scavenger, or a good surgeon. You see at once that education is essentially for freemen and vocational training for slaves. That is how they were distributed in the old unequal societies; the poor man's son was apprenticed to a trade, the rich man's son went to Eton and Oxford and then made the grand tour. When societies become, in effort if not in achievement, egalitarian, we are presented with a difficulty. To give every one education and to give no one vocational training is impossible, for electricians and surgeons we must have and they must be trained. Our ideal must be to find time for both education and training: our danger is that equality may mean training for all and education for none—that every one will learn commercial French instead of Latin, book-keeping instead of geometry, and 'knowledge of the world we live in' instead of great literature. It is against this danger that schoolmasters have to fight, for if education is beaten by training, civilization dies. That is a thing very likely to happen. One of the most dangerous errors instilled into us by nineteenth-century progressive optimism is the idea that civilization is automatically bound to increase and spread. The lesson of history is the opposite; civilization is a rarity, attained with difficulty and easily lost. The normal state of humanity is barbarism, just as the normal surface of our planet is salt water. Land looms large in our imagination of the planet and civilization in our history books, only because sea and savagery are,

to us, less interesting. And if you press to know what
I mean by civilization, I reply 'Humanity', by which
I do not mean kindness so much as the realization of
the human idea. Human life means to me the life of
beings for whom the leisured activities of thought,
art, literature, conversation are the end,[1] and the
preservation and propagation of life merely the
means. That is why education seems to me so important: it actualizes that potentiality for leisure, if you
like for amateurishness, which is man's prerogative.
You have noticed, I hope, that man is the only
amateur animal; all the others are professionals.
They have no leisure and do not desire it. When the
cow has finished eating she chews the cud; when she
has finished chewing she sleeps; when she has finished
sleeping she eats again. She is a machine for turning
grass into calves and milk—in other words, for producing more cows. The lion cannot stop hunting,
nor the beaver building dams, nor the bee making
honey. When God made the beasts dumb He saved
the world from infinite boredom, for if they could
speak they would all of them, all day, talk nothing
but shop.

That is my idea of education. You see at once that
it implies an immense superiority on the part of the
teacher. He is trying to make the pupil a good man,
in the sense I have described. The assumption is that
the master is already human, the pupil a mere candidate for humanity—an unregenerate little bundle of

---

[1] The natural end. It would have been out of place here to say what I
believe about Man's supernatural end or to explain why I think the natural
end should be pursued although, in isolation from the supernatural, it
cannot be fully realized.

appetites which is to be kneaded and moulded into
human shape by one who knows better. In education
the master is the agent, the pupil, the patient.

Now learning, considered in itself, has, on my view,
no connexion at all with education. It is an activity
for men—that is for beings who have already been
humanized by this kneading and moulding process.
Among these men—these biologically simian animals
who have been made into men—there are some who
desire to know. Or rather, all desire to know, but
some desire it more fervently than the majority and
are ready to make greater sacrifices for it. The things
they want to know may be quite different. One may
want to know what happened a million years ago,
another, what happens a million light-years away,
a third, what is happening in his own table on the
microscopic level. What is common to them all is the
thirst for knowledge. Now it might have happened
that such people were left in civil societies to gratify
their taste as best they could without assistance or
interference from their fellows. It has not happened.
Such societies have usually held a belief—and it is a
belief of a quite transcendental nature—that knowledge is the natural food of the human mind: that
those who specially pursue it are being specially
human; and that their activity is good in itself besides
being always honourable and sometimes useful to
the whole society. Hence we come to have such
associations as universities—institutions for the support and encouragement of men devoted to learning.

You have doubtless been told—but it can hardly
be repeated too often—that our colleges at Oxford

were founded not in order to teach the young but in order to support masters of arts. In their original institution they are homes not for teaching but for the pursuit of knowledge; and their original nature is witnessed by the brute fact that hardly any college in Oxford is financially dependent on the under-graduates' fees, and that most colleges are content if they do not lose over the undergraduate. A school without pupils would cease to be school; a college without undergraduates would be as much a college as ever, would perhaps be more a college.

It follows that the university student is essentially a different person from the school pupil. He is not a candidate for humanity, he is, in theory, already human. He is not a patient; nor is his tutor an operator who is doing something to him. The student is, or ought to be, a young man who is already begin-ning to follow learning for its own sake, and who attaches himself to an older student, not precisely to be taught, but to pick up what he can. From the very beginning the two ought to be fellow students. And that means they ought not to be thinking about each other but about the subject. The schoolmaster must think about the pupil: everything he says is said to improve the boy's character or open his mind—the schoolmaster is there to make the pupil a 'good' man. And the pupil must think about the master. Obedi-ence is one of the virtues he has come to him to learn; his motive for reading one book and neglecting another must constantly be that he was told to. But the elder student has no such duties *ex officio* to the younger. His business is to pursue knowledge. If his pursuit happens to be helpful to the junior partner, he is welcome to be present; if not, he is welcome to stay at home. No doubt the elder, of his charity, may go a little out of his course to help the younger; but he is then acting as a man, not as a student.

Such is the ideal. In fact, of course, Oxford has become in modern times very largely a place of teaching. I spend most of the term teaching and my tutorial stipend is a part of my income no less important than my fellowship. Most of you, perhaps, have come here with the idea of completing your education rather than with the idea of entering a society devoted to the pursuit of knowledge for its own sake. What do these changes mean? They mean, I think, that a temporary immersion in the life of learning has been found to have an educational value. Learning is not education; but it can be used educationally by those who do not propose to pursue learning all their lives. There is nothing odd in the existence of such a by-product. Games are essentially for pleasure, but they happen to produce health. They are not likely, however, to produce health if they are played for the sake of it. Play to win and you will find yourself taking violent exercise; play because it is good for you and you will not. In the same way, though you may have come here only to be educated, you will never receive that precise educational gift which a university has to give you unless you can at least *pretend*, so long as you are with us, that you are concerned not with education but with knowledge for its own sake. And we, on our part, can do very little for you if we aim directly at your education. We assume that you are already human, already good men; that you have the specifically human virtues and above all the great virtue of curiosity. We are not going to try to improve you; we have fulfilled our whole function if we help you to *see* some given tract of reality.

I dare say some of you are wondering by now what all this has to do with the English syllabus. I am just coming to that. From what I have said, it follows that on my view a freshman hesitating over the choice of a Final School is quite on the wrong track if he is asking himself, 'Which gives me the best general education?' He may be compelled to ask, 'Which qualifies me for the best jobs when I go down?' for unfortunately we have to make our livings. The necessity which thus limits his choice is, as it were, an external necessity: poverty will prevent one man from becoming an astronomer as blindness may prevent another from becoming a painter. But to ask for the best 'general education' is to ask for one's schooldays over again. The proper question for a freshman is not 'What will do me most good?' but 'What do I most want to know?' For nothing that we have to offer will do him good unless he can be persuaded to forget all about self-improvement for three or four years, and to absorb himself in getting to know some part of reality, as it is in itself.

The qualification 'as it is in itself' is here important. At first sight it might seem that since the student cannot study everything he should at least study a bit of everything; that the best Final Honour School would have a composite syllabus—a little philosophy, a little politics, a little economics, a little science, a little literature. There are many objections to such a discipline, but I will mention that one only which is central to my argument. The composite school, as its very name implies, has been composed by some one. Those little bits of various subjects are not found lying together in those quantities and in that order which the syllabus shows. They have been put together in that way artificially by a committee of professors. That committee cannot have been following the grain and joint of reality as reality discovers itself to those actually engaged in the pursuit of learning. For the life of learning knows nothing of this nicely balanced encyclopaedic arrangement. Every one of the suggested subjects is infinite and, in its own way, covers the whole field of reality. The committee would in fact be guided by their idea of what would do the students good—that is, by a purely educational idea. In reading such a school, therefore, you would not be turned loose on some tract of reality as it is, to make what you could of it; you would be getting selections of reality selected by your elders—something cooked, expurgated, filtered, and generally toned down for your edification. You would still be in the leading strings and might as well have stayed at school. Your whole reading in its scope and proportions would bear the impress neither of reality nor of your own mind but of the mind of the committee. The educational ideals of a particular age, class, and philosophy of life would be stamped on your whole career.

The objection will naturally be clearest to us if we consider how the subject we know best would fare in such a school. There would be a little bit of literature. What would it consist of? Obviously, of great works, for we should have to make up in quality what we lacked in quantity. Perhaps a few great 'classics' each from French, German, and English. As a curriculum for a schoolboy, nothing could be more liberal and edifying. But you see at once that it has very little to do with a knowledge of literature as it really grows and works, with all its ups and downs, in any actual country. It may train your mind and make you in the Aristotelian sense a better man; but are you not old enough now to cease being trained? Is it not time for you to venture to look on reality in the raw?

If this objection to the composite school is accepted, we may summarily reject certain proposals for the reform of the English School. When people ask, 'Why not a little philosophy?' 'Why not Italian literature?' 'Why not some psychology?', they are usually hankering after the composite school. But they may have better motives than that. They may want philosophy and Italian not because these are educational but because English writers have in fact been influenced by philosophical speculation and by Italian literature—because these things, in fact, *are* parts of the piece of reality we have set out to study.

They are quite right. So is the history of the Romance and Germanic languages from the earliest times, the history of all the literatures that have affected us, the history, political, social, and economic, of all Europe, and even the flora, fauna, and geology of Great Britain. A perfect study of English would involve all this; nay, as Hegel saw, a perfect study of anything requires a knowledge of everything. But

The lyf so short, the craft so long to lerne

forces us to be content with less, and you, who are with us for only four years, to be content with less still. Thus I admit that some limitation is necessary; the whole literary reality cannot be embraced by any Final Honour School. But there is a difference between arbitrary selection and a curtailment which obediently follows the joints of the real as they are, not as we choose to pretend they are. Thus if a man has not time to learn the geography of the world, we might teach him that of Great Britain, a land mass given to us by nature. There are facts about England which he would be unable to understand because he did not know Europe; we should have to put up with that. The other, the arbitrary, alternative would be to give him selected high lights from all over the planet—the Grand Canyon, the Rhine, a glimpse of a South American forest, the Bay of Biscay, and the Gobi Desert. The first would give him a real though limited knowledge of nature—would teach him how one country smelled, looked, lived, and died. But the second might make him a mere globe trotter.

In this spirit then, we approach our vast subject of English literature, admitting that we cannot study it whole, but determined to neglect outlying provinces and remote connexions rather than to break up the central unity. The first thing to do, obviously, is to cut off some years from this end. The reasons for choosing this end are, I suppose, obvious. In the first

place, we naturally wish to help the students in study-
ing those parts of the subject where we have most help
to give and they need help most. On recent and contemporary literature their need is least and our help
least. They ought to understand it better than we,
and if they do not then there is something radically
wrong either with them or with the literature. But
I need not labour the point. There is an intrinsic
absurdity in making current literature a subject of
academic study, and the student who wants a tutor's
assistance in reading the works of his own contemporaries might as well ask for a nurse's assistance in
blowing his own nose. Again, things are understood
by what precedes them rather than by what follows
them. It may be disappointing to stop a story in the
middle, but you can understand it as far as you have
gone; you cannot understand it if you *begin* in the
middle. I can indeed imagine a man denying this
and maintaining that the nineteenth century can be
understood only in the light of the twentieth. But if
that is so, then the twentieth can be understood only
in the light of the twenty-first and all succeeding
centuries. We are therefore doomed to an equal
misunderstanding wherever we stop, and may just
as well stop where we find it convenient.

We begin then by cutting off a hundred, or two
hundred, or any reasonable number of years from
this end, and still we have too much left. If we picture
our subject as a tree we have first of all the soil in
which it grows: that is, the history of the English
people, social, economic, and intellectual. I imagine
that neither you nor I wish to draw attention to this;

for if you look in the statutes you will find that exami-
ners are at liberty to set questions on it, and it is
always possible that if we talk much about it they
may wake up and really do so. Let us keep quiet
about the soil, and go on to the roots. The great
central tap-root is old Germanic developing, as we
pass above the ground-level, into Old English. A
second root, not quite so big and important as this,
is Old French. A third, noticeably smaller, strikes
farther away into Latin. But all these are pretty
tough and more or less essential to the tree. Then
come the little ones—the tiny, much advertised, and
attractive Greek root, the modern Spanish, modern
Italian, modern French, German, &c. Our problem
is to find which of these we can neglect with least
violence to the nature of the tree.

Well—the little ones must go. We have not time,
in four years, for Greek, Spanish, Italian, French,
and German. If one could be saved, it would have to
be modern French. Of course if we were considering
which is the most interesting in itself I should unhesi-
tatingly choose the Greek; but that would be to fall
back from naturalism to arbitrary selection, from
learning to education. Certainly Greek literature is
better than French; but certainly English and French
lie together in reality as English and Greek do not.
But even French we can hardly save, for we have the
three great roots to consider. The tap-root, Anglo-
Saxon, can never be abandoned. The man who does
not know it remains all his life a child among real
English students. There we find the speech-rhythms
that we use every day made the basis of metre; there

we find the origins of that romanticism for which the ignorant invent such odd explanations. This is our own stuff and its life is in every branch of the tree to the remotest twigs. That we cannot abandon. Old French and Latin we have reluctantly given up: if you want them, I am the last man to deny you.

With these limitations, then, we hand you over our tract of reality. Do not be deceived by talk about the narrowness of the specialist. The opposite of the specialist, as you now see, is the student enslaved to some one else's selection. In the great rough countryside which we throw open to you, you can choose your own path. Here's your gun, your spade, your fishing-tackle; go and get yourself a dinner. Do not tell me that you would sooner have a nice composite *menu* of dishes from half the world drawn up for you. You are too old for that. It is time you learned to wrestle with nature for yourself. And whom will you trust to draw up the *menu*? How do you know that in that very river which I would exclude as poisonous the fish you specially want, the undiscovered fish, is waiting? And you would never find it if you let us select. *Our* selection would be an effort to bind the future within *our* present knowledge and taste: nothing more could come out than we had put in. It would be worse; it would be a kind of propaganda, concealed, unconscious, and omnipotent. Is it really true that you would prefer that to the run of your teeth over the whole country? Have you no incredulity, no scepticism, left?

V

HIGH AND LOW BROWS

Quick, quick.—Fling *Peregrine Pickle* under the toilet—throw *Roderick Random* into the closet—put *The Innocent Adultery* into *The Whole Duty of Man*—cram *Ovid* behind the bolster—there —put *The Man of Feeling* into your pocket—so, so—now lay *Mrs. Chapone* in sight, and leave Fordyce's *Sermons* open on the table.

SHERIDAN

Read to the English Society at Oxford

HIGH AND LOW BROWS

ARISTOTLE often begins his argument with what he calls an Isagoge, a collection of instances which is not, if I understand the matter, intended (like Mill's induction) to prove a general principle, but merely to open our eyes to it. The following instances are meant to form such an isagoge.

1. Not many years ago a lady whose studies I was attempting to supervise, propounded a literary theory of general application which I found myself unable to accept. Applying the elenchus after my fashion I inquired whether her theory would cover *The Tale of Peter Rabbit*. After a silence of some minutes, she asked me if I thought there was any use in introducing such an example into a serious literary discussion. I replied that *Peter Rabbit* was a book and certainly not so bad a book that it could be left outside the classification 'literature'. The lady, who is as honest as she is learned (and whom I mention here with all respect), was not prepared to call *Peter Rabbit* 'bad'. 'Trivial' was the word she finally fixed on. But she was quite sure that doctrines about 'literature' need not apply to it.

2. I have heard of a preparatory school where the library regulations divide the contents of the library into two classes: Good Books and Books. The boys are allowed to take out two Good Books for every one Book. To read a Good Book is meritorious, to read a Book only tolerable. At the same time, those responsible for the regulations have hesitated to

label as 'bad' the books which they thus contrast with the 'good'.

3. I have heard the Head of a great college[1] praise the novels of Anthony Hope and conclude by declaring with enthusiasm, 'They are the best "bad" books I've ever read'. Here, it will be seen, the word 'bad' is actually used but used in a sense which admits, inside the class Bad, distinctions of good, better, and best.

4. I have often heard—and who has not?—a plain man praise even to rapture the delightful merits of some favourite story and end with the humble reservation, 'Of course, I know it's not real literature'.

I trust that these four instances are already making clear to you what it is I want to discuss. In all of them we see a distinction made between two kinds of book, to the one of which a certain honour is attached, and to the other a certain note of ignomi
ny. Yet in spite of this there is a reluctance to identify this distinction with the plain distinctions of good from bad or better from worse. Those who uphold the distinction prefer to call the inferior class popular, common, commercial, cheap, trashy, or the like, and the superior class literary, classical, serious, or artistic. In our own time the two odious adjectives *Lowbrow* and *Highbrow* have been introduced as the names of the two classes and bid fair to oust all their rivals. There will also be noticed in the first, third, and fourth of my instances a suggestion that the lowbrow works are so different

[1] I have learned since that I misunderstood him, but as my Isagoge is meant for pure illustration, not proof, I have thought it no dishonesty to let the example stand.

in kind from the highbrow that they have a goodness
and badness of their own, a servile virtue and servile
vice peculiar to themselves, that they are to be judged
by peculiar standards, and that what is said of literature *simpliciter* is not said of them.

Now it seems to me that in this popular distinction
there is some confusion between degrees and kinds of
merit. If the *lowbrow* books are really a special kind
of book I do not see how they can be inferior to the
high. You cannot be beaten by a man unless you
enter the same competition with him, nor overtaken
by a man (as Chesterton observes) unless you both
run in the same direction. At present the distinction
is certainly used to allow us the satisfaction of despis-
ing certain authors and readers without imposing
on us the labour of showing that they are bad. It is
also used, I find, to allow people to enjoy lowbrow
art without gratitude on the one hand or shame on
the other, and those who would hesitate to say, 'Let's
go and see something bad' will cheerfully say 'Let's
go to a lowbrow film'. The whole distinction seems to
be made in order to enable us to have it both ways.

In the following paper I propose two questions.
(1) Is the class of lowbrow books (or 'books' simply
as at the Preparatory School) really the class of bad
books? (2) If not, is the distinction useful in some
other way?

As soon as we approach the first question we notice
that even if all the lowbrow books—which I am going
to call Class A—are in fact bad, even so the distinction
between lowbrow and highbrow—or between class A
and class B—will not coincide with the distinction

between bad books and good books, for the very
obvious reason that class B contains bad books too.
Gorboduc and Glover's *Leonidas* and Dyer's *Fleece*,
Gabriel Harvey's hexameters and Johnson's *Irene*,
Tennyson's tragedies and Southey's epics—all these
are classical enough, serious enough, and literary
enough, in all conscience. If they entered the school
library it would certainly be as Good Books, not as
Books. And it will hardly be denied that some of
them are bad. In fact, as soon as we look at the question from this point of view, it becomes apparent that
class A is not simply the class of bad books. Mere
failure does not infallibly give the right of entry to it.
If all the books in it are bad it must be with some
special sort of badness—an A badness.

But are they all bad? As I have not read the novels
of Anthony Hope, I cannot, though my third instance
invites me, select them for analysis; but perhaps
Rider Haggard will do as well, for his books are certainly in the A class and, in my opinion, some of them
are good—are therefore 'good "bad" books' as the
Head of that college would say. And of his books I
select *She*. If I ask myself why it is that I have more
than once read *She* with enjoyment, I find that there
is every reason why I should have done so. In the
first place the story makes an excellent approach; the
central theme is suffered, in the first chapters, to woo
us across great distances of space and time. What we
are presently to see at close quarters is seen at first,
as it were, through the wrong end of the telescope.
This is a fine exercise in the art of alluring—you may
see the same thing at work in the opening of the

Utopia, in the second act of *Prometheus Unbound*, and
in the early books of the *Odyssey*. In the second place
it is a quest story, which is an attractive thing. And
the object of the quest combines two strong appeals—
it is the 'fountain of youth' theme and the *princesse
lointaine* in one. Finally, the withdrawal or conclusion, which is always the difficulty in quest stories, is
effected by unexpected means which are nevertheless, on the author's suppositions, sufficiently plau-
sible. In the conduct of the story the detail is mostly
convincing. The characters who are meant to be
amiable are amiable and those who are meant to be
sinister are sinister. The goodness of *She* is grounded,
as firmly as that of any book whatever, on the fundamental laws of the imagination. But there is badness
in it as well as goodness. Two things deter us from
regarding it as a quite satisfactory romance. One of
them is the continuous poverty of the style, by which,
of course, I do not mean any failure to conform to
certain *a priori* rules, but rather a sloth or incom-
petence of writing whereby the author is content
always with a vague approximation to the emotion,
the reflection, or the image he intends, so that a
certain smudging and banality is spread over all.
The other fault is the shallowness and folly of the
things put into the mouth of She herself and offered
us for wisdom. That She, in her secular loneliness,
should have become a sage, is very proper, and
indeed essential to Haggard's story, but Haggard has
not himself the wisdom wherewith to supply her. A
poet of Dante's depth could have given her things
really wise to say; a poet of Shakespeare's address

would have made us believe in her wisdom without committing himself.

If my analysis is correct, *She* is not a 'good "bad" book' in the sense of being a good specimen of a bad kind; it is simply good and bad, like many other books, in the sense that it is good in some respects and bad in others. And those who have read it with enjoyment have been enjoying real literary merits, and merits which it shares with the *Odyssey* or *The Life and Death of Jason*. Certainly, it is not a *very* good book, but since its vices are not sufficient to overwhelm its virtues (as the experience of many wiser readers than I has proved) it is better, say, than *Leonidas* or the *Epic of Hades*. In other words, this book of the A class is better than some books of the B class. It is better by every test; it shows more skill in the author and produces more pleasure in the reader; it is more in touch with the permanent nature of our imagination; it leaves those who have read it richer. And with this, the attempt to identify the classes A and B with the classes bad and good or worse and better has surely collapsed.

We must now cast about for some other possible definition of the two classes; and it comes at once into my mind that the lady in my first instance ruled *Peter Rabbit* out as 'trivial'. Perhaps the A class consists of trivial, and the B class of grave, or weighty, or momentous books. I think that those who use the A–B antithesis very often have something of this sort in their mind, but it is difficult to fix the exact sense of any of the words they use to express it. It is clear that the contrast cannot be simply between comic and serious, for then the stories in our Parish Magazine would be labelled B and *Le Misanthrope*, A. It might be argued, no doubt, that Molière's play, though comic, is momentous as touching life at many points and dealing with the depths of our nature, and this might furnish the ground for a restatement of the distinction—B books being 'momentous' in the sense just suggested, while A books touch us only superficially, or concern only highly specialized areas of our consciousness. But this would make *The Importance of Being Earnest* an A. Nor is it clear that all the books already in the A class are thus superficial. They are often accused of being 'sentimental'; and this charge, on inspection, often conceals an admission that their appeal is to emotions very basic and universal—to the same emotions that are concerned in great tragedies. Even Dr. Richards's *Boosey Ballad*,[1] which is not only A but bad simply, has a theme that Petrarch might not have disdained. Indeed, the more I look into it the more I am convinced that any contrast of weighty and frivolous, solid and slight, deep and shallow, must cut right across the A and B distinction. How many of the most perfect things are, after all, trifles! The weighty and frivolous are kinds of literature, and in each kind we shall find good A's, bad A's, good B's, and bad B's. This is not what we are looking for.

Among the lowbrows themselves I find that the distinction is often based on style. When the plain man confesses that the books he delights in are not 'real Literature' he will often, if pressed, explain this

---

[1] See his *Principles of Literary Criticism*, cap. 24.

by saying that they 'haven't got style' or 'style and all that'. And when the plain man has been captured and made into a pathetically willing and bewildered university student he will sometimes praise the great works which he has dutifully read and not enjoyed, for the excellence of their style. He has missed the jokes in the comedy, remained unmoved by the tragedy, failed to respond to the suggestions of the lyric, and found the episodes of the romance uninteresting; utterly at a loss to explain the value traditionally set on what has proved to him so tedious, he hands it over to the thing he knows least about, to a mysterious entity called Style, which is to him merely what occult forces were to the old scientists—an *asylum ignorantiae*. He does so because he has a radically false conception of style. He thinks of it not as the linguistic means by which the writer produces whatever results he desires but as a sort of extra— an uncovenanted pedantry tacked on to the book proper, to gratify some specifically 'literary' or 'critical' taste which has nothing to do with the ordinary pleasures of the imagination. It is for him a meaningless addition which, by a convention, gives access to a higher rank—like the letters Esq. after a man's name on an envelope. Now it must be confessed that the highbrows sometimes talk of style in a way which gives their weaker brethren some excuse for such misconceptions; but I think that most of them, in a cool hour, would admit that 'Style', in the sense in which the lowbrow uses the word, does not exist. When we say that the descriptions of country in *She* are marred by their deficiency of style, we do not mean (as the ignorant suppose) that they are good as descriptions but lacking in some abstractly 'literary' and undescriptive grace which might have been superadded; we mean that they are imperfect descriptions; and we call their imperfection 'stylistic' because it is due not to faults in the author's conception but to his careless or insensitive language. A better choice of epithets, and those distant mountains would have stood out sharper on the horizon; a well chosen metaphor, and the whole picture, now dimly discerned through seas of wasteful words, would have printed itself for ever on the inner eye; a nobler rhythm, and the sense of space and movement would have been given us, not left, as it now is, for us to infer. Turn from *She* to almost any page in *Eothen*, and you will soon see what style in a descriptive passage means. There is no class of books which can be 'good in their own way' without bothering about style. There are books in which what the author is saying imperfectly, partly failing to say, is sufficiently interesting to keep us reading in spite of his failure. Though he has done only half his work, we are content to do some of it for him. Such books are books defective in style. And they do not come only in class A. Scott, Dickens, Byron, Spenser, Alanus, and Apuleius have detestable faults of style, but they are usually put in class B. St. Paul, despite some passages of striking beauty, seems to me to write badly, but he is hardly an A; and I have found in the style of Donne, Chapman, Meredith, Saintsbury, and others, obstacles to the enjoyment of what they have to give me as great as those I find in Rider Haggard. It is not important here that any reader should agree with the instances I am choosing; what matters is the recognition that badness of style (like triviality) will be found in B books. It cannot be made the basis of a dichotomy between two kinds of book.

Another common way of using the distinction tends to fix on 'popular' as the best adjective for class A. 'Popular' art is supposed to aim at mere *entertainment*, while 'real' or 'serious' art aims at some specifically 'artistic' or 'aesthetic' or even 'spiritual' satisfaction. This is an attractive view because it would give those who hold it a ground for maintaining that popular literature has its own good and bad, according to its own rules, distinct from those of Literature proper. The popular novel aiming only at passing the reader's time, the popular comedy content to raise a laugh, and be forgotten, the popular tragedy which only wants to give us 'a good cry', would have their low, separate, legitimate places. And since I observe that many of my highest-browed acquaintances spend much of their time in talking of the vulgarity of popular art, and therefore must know it well, and could not have acquired that knowledge unless they enjoyed it, I must assume that they would welcome a theory which justified them in drinking freely of that fountain without forfeiting their superiority. But there is a troublesome difficulty in this form of the distinction. We know, without going to look, that the Good Books in that preparatory school library would include the novels of Scott and Dickens. But these, in their own day, were popular *entertainment*, best sellers. Some of the contemporary highbrows

may retort that they ought never to have been
allowed into the B class. I do not agree, but let us
concede it. Let us even concede the same about
Scott's poems, and about Byron, which were also
once A's and are now B's. But what of Fielding, of
Malory, of Shakespeare and all his colleagues? Of
the metrical romances? Of Ovid, scribbled on the
walls at Pompeii? What of Molière, finding the best
judge of his work in the old woman who never
failed to laugh in the same place as the audience—
the audience whom he wrote to please? What, in
another art, of Mozart's operas? It is not sufficient to
say that a work designed for the popular market may
sometimes, by a happy freak, outshoot its mark. The
thing has happened too often to be called a freak.
What survives from most ages is chiefly either the
work that had some religious or national appeal, or
else the popular, commercial work produced for
entertainment. I say 'chiefly' because the work of
the 'pure' artists is not always ephemeral; a little, a
very little, of it survives. But the great mass of literature which now fills class B is the work of men who
wrote either piously, to edify their fellows, or com-
mercially, to earn their living by 'giving the public
what it wanted'.

This leads to the very interesting conclusion that
the B's of one age have most often been the A's of
another. We are sometimes warned by the supporters
of difficult new movements in literature not to imitate
our fathers in stoning the prophets; those who dislike
Pound or Joyce are told 'so you would have disliked
Wordsworth and Shelley if you had lived then'. The

warning may be useful, but clearly it should be
supplemented by another—'Beware how you scorn
the best sellers of to-day; they may be classics for the
intelligentsia of the Twenty-Third Century.'

If our age is known to posterity not as that of Eliot
and Auden but as that of Buchan and Wodehouse
(and stranger things have come to pass), Buchan and
Wodehouse will then be B's and little boys will get
good marks for reading them. Shakespeare and
Scott, once A's, are now B's. If we could find what it
is that the mere passage of time does to a book, we
should have found out something about the real
nature of the A and B distinction. And surely, it is
obvious that what time does to a book is to make it
difficult. There are indeed other operations of time.
It makes a book more widely known or spreads on it
that rich patina we now enjoy in Virgil or Malory;
but neither of these would furnish the basis for a B
class since this is to include contemporary books as
well. We want a quality which some books have at
once but which mere time can confer on books that
originally lacked it; and difficulty seems to be the
quality required. It would be amusing if difficulty
turned out to be the real criterion of Literature,
Good Books, or classics—if a comedy which was
mere commercial art as long as every one could see
the jokes became aesthetic and spiritual as soon as
you need commentators to explain them. Yet I think
this comes much nearer to the ground of the distinction actually made than any of the hypotheses we
have yet discussed.

A distinction simply between easy and difficult

books is a reasonable one; and it is certainly better to be able to enjoy both kinds than to be limited to the easy. A man who has hitherto relished only the easy and now learns to relish the difficult as well, may properly be said to have improved his taste, for enlargement, other things being equal, is improvement. But there is a great difference between improvement in this sense—the mere enlargement of a taste which may already have been perfectly good within its own limits—and improvement in the sense of correction or of conversion from the bad to the good. There is also a great difference between the easy and the bad. No book can be bad because it is easy or good because it is hard: a book may be bad because it is hard. If ease and difficulty is the real antithesis behind the A and B distinction, then the distinction is being widely misused and from the true premise 'it is better to advance to the difficult books (without leaving the easy ones) if you can' some draw the false conclusions that the difficult books are better and that you can advance to them only by leaving the easy ones behind. We shall see presently the psychological causes of this error.

Closely connected with this form of the distinction is that other which makes 'vulgarity' the criterion of an A book. It might be sufficient in answer to this to inquire what sense can possibly be given to the word Vulgar which will apply to the work of Beatrix Potter, John Buchan, George Birmingham, P. G. Wodehouse, 'Somerville and Ross', and a dozen more writers of the A class. But Vulgar is a word so difficult and, in our days, so ubiquitous that perhaps we should examine it more closely. It seems to me to have two principal meanings. In its first sense it is a purely privative term meaning 'not refined', 'not subtle or delicate or many sided'. What is vulgar in this sense (cf. 'the vulgar tongue') may be perfectly good: to lack refinement or subtlety when refinement or subtlety are not required is no blemish. Thus the line

> Then come kiss me, sweet and twenty

is, in its context, good and yet 'vulgar' because it expresses a conception of love neither elevated nor discriminating, and this is all that the song requires. The very same line would be vulgar in a bad sense if any one were absurd enough to put it into the mouth of Launcelot addressing Guinevere after he has broken the bars or Zeus addressing Danae as he emerges from the shower of gold. From this point of view we might admit that all A literature is and ought to be irreproachably 'vulgar'. It ought to deal strongly and simply with strong, simple emotions: the directness, the unelaborate, downright portraiture of easily recognizable realities in their familiar aspects, will not be a fault unless it pretends to be something else. If it essays, without delicacy, that which demands delicacy, it will then become faultily vulgar; but the whole art of good A writers stands upon not doing so. But there is a second sense of Vulgar; it may be used to mean something essentially and, in the long run, morally, bad: the base, the mean, the ignoble. These terms themselves are ambiguous, but perhaps an example will make the matter clear. The best instance I know of Vulgarity

in this evil sense occurs in Chapman's *Iliad*. Homer
has said of the old men on the wall,

οἱ δ'ὥς οὖν εἴδονθ' Ἑλένην ἐπὶ πύργον ἰοῦσαν,
ἦκα πρὸς ἀλλήλους ἔπεα πτερόεντ' ἀγόρευον.

Chapman translates

when they saw the power
Of beauty, in the queen, ascend, even those *cold-spirited*
peers,
Those wise and almost withered men, found *this heat* in
their years
That they *were forced* (though whispering) to say, &c.

I do not mean, of course, that the suggestion of senile
eroticism which Chapman has foisted on the original
is in itself and necessarily vulgar; a man might make
good lines, whether comic or tragic, even on this subject. But to have let it creep in here of all places, to
be unaware of gulfs of difference between this and
anything Homer need be supposed to have meant,
argues an ungentle heart and a bestial ignorance of
the whole hierarchy of human feelings. It is something more than lack of delicacy where delicacy is
required (though of course it is that too); it is a fatal,
unconscious welcome held out to the lower when the
lower has offered to usurp the place of the higher, 'a
downward appetite to mix with mud'. And we cannot here avoid such words as Lower and Higher, for
Vulgar, in its deeper sense, is really a term of moral
reproof. It has nothing to do with the distinction of
popular and classic. It is low hearts and not low
brows that are vulgar.[1]

---

[1] Another example, more venial, but perhaps even clearer, of such vulgarity, occurs when Dryden renders *Quare agite, o tectis, iuvenes, succedite nostris*

We have now made a fairly determined effort to
find some useful meaning for the separation of literature into the two classes of classical and popular,
Good Books and Books, literary and commercial,
highbrow and lowbrow, and we have failed. In fact,
the distinction rests upon a confusion between degrees
of merit and differences of kind. Our map of literature has been made to look like an examination list—
a single column of names with a horizontal line
drawn across it, the honour candidates above that
line, and the pass candidates below it. But we ought
rather to have a whole series of vertical lines representing different kinds of work, and an almost infinite
series of horizontal lines crossing these to represent
the different degrees of goodness in each kind. Thus
'Simple Adventure Story' is a vertical line with the
Odyssey at the top and Edgar Wallace at the bottom;
Rider Haggard, R. L. Stevenson, Scott, William
Morris will be placed on horizontal lines crossing
'Adventure Story' at such heights as we may decide.
'Psychological Story' is a separate column, with its
own top (Tolstoy or another) and its own bottom.
With such a picture in our minds we should avoid
the confusion of those who say to a boy, 'You should
not read trash like *King Solomon's Mines.* Try Meredith.' Such an exhortation urges him in two quite
different directions. You are asking him at once to
move horizontally, from one kind to another, and
vertically, from the less good to the better. But you
are also doing something worse; you are instilling

(*Aen.* i. 627), 'Enter, my noble guest, and you shall find, If not a costly
welcome, yet a kind.' The descent here is to the 'genteel'. Cf. Gavin
Douglas's excellent version of the same line.

into his mind a notion (often henceforward indelible) that the pleasure he already has in not very good books is of a quite different nature from anything he is to expect in 'real literature'—that the latter is something to be read 'in school', an affair of marks and School Certificates and conceit and self-improvement.

I believe that this misconception is likely to grow and to be one day no longer confined to schoolboys. There are many circumstances which encourage it. Until quite modern times the reading of imaginative literature in a man's own tongue was not regarded as meritorious. The great authors of the past wrote to entertain the leisure of their adult contemporaries, and a man who cared for literature needed no spur and expected no good conduct marks for sitting down to the food provided for him. Boys at school were taught to read Latin and Greek poetry by the birch, and discovered the English poets as accidentally and naturally as they now discover the local cinema. Most of my own generation, and many, I hope, of yours, tumbled into literature in that fashion. Of each of us some great poet made a rape when we still wore Eton collars. Shall we be thought immodest if we claim that most of the books we loved from the first were good books and our earliest loves are still unrepented? If so, that very fact bears witness to the novelty of the modern situation; to us, the claim that we have always liked Keats is no prouder than the claim that we have always liked bacon and eggs.

For there are changes afoot. The growth of English Schools at Universities, the School Certificate, and

I

the Educational Ladder—all excellent things—may yet produce unexpected results. I foresee the growth of a new race of readers and critics to whom, from the very outset, good literature will be an accomplishment rather than a delight, and who will always feel, beneath the acquired taste, the backward tug of something else which they feel merit in resisting. Such people will not be content to say that some books are bad or not very good; they will make a special class of 'lowbrow' art which is to be vilified, mocked, quarantined, and sometimes (when they are sick or tired) enjoyed. They will be sure that what is popular must always be bad, thus assuming that human taste is *naturally* wrong, that it needs not only improvement and development but veritable conversion. For them a good critic will be, as the theologians say, essentially a 'twice-born' critic, one who is regenerate and washed from his Original Taste. They will have no conception, because they have had no experience, of spontaneous delight in excellence. Their 'good' taste will have been acquired by the sweat of their brows, its acquisition will often (and legitimately) have coincided with advancement in the social and economic scale, and they will hold it with uneasy intensity. As they will be contemptuous of popular books, so they will be naïvely tolerant of dullness and difficulty in any quack or sloven who comes before them with lofty pretensions; *all* literature having been as hard to them as that, as much an acquired taste, they will not see the difference. They will be angry with a true lover of literature who does not take pains to unravel

the latest poetical puzzle, and call him a *dilettante*.
Having obtained the freedom of Parnassus at a great
price, they will be unable to endure the nonchalance
of those who were free-born.

The cure for this is not to remove the Educational
Ladder, the English Schools, nor the Certificate
examinations. If the danger is recognized it can be
combated by teaching and by criticism at every
point. Those in the predicament I have described
can combat it in themselves if they will. A very little
attention will soon discover in any 'lowbrow' book
what is really good and really bad, and will show us
the very same kinds of goodness and badness in books
that are not lowbrow. A little patience, a little humi-
lity, and all will be well. It is the vanity of new
acquisitions and the lazy desire for over-simplification
which threatens to impound a hundred books, some
irredeemably bad, some excellently good, in a class
which can be dismissed from criticism. A man ought
not to be ashamed of reading a good book because it
is simple and popular, and he ought not to condone
the faults of a bad book because it is simple and
popular. He should be able to say (altering the names
to suit his own judgement), 'I read Buchan and Eliot
for the same reason, because I think them good; I
leave Edgar Wallace and Ezra Pound unread for the
same reason, because I think them bad.' It is by no
means for the protection of bad books that I wish the
distinction of high- and lowbrow abolished. That
distinction itself protects bad books. As it robs excellent A books of deserved praise, it teaches its victims
to tolerate bad A books. Why was Dr. Richards

reading a bad book when he had influenza?[1] Was it not that in his illness he needed an easy book, and having lumped all easy books together as contemptible, he made no further distinctions? That is the usual result of having a pariah class. Slavery, while depressing the slave of noble character, allows the vile slave liberties never conceded to the free servant. Those who most despise the class from which prostitutes are recruited are not necessarily those who abstain from fornication. And indeed, I am often shocked at what slips out sometimes about the recreational reading, the off-duty intellectual amusements, of those who are sternest in their contempt for popular art and demand least pleasure of the art they approve.[2]

[1] See *Practical Criticism* (1929), p. 257. I am sorry to have to mention in this context an admission whose candour deserves so much imitation and a critic whose works are almost the necessary starting-point for all future literary theory. But the point is very important, and *magis amica veritas*.

[2] A full treatment of the subject broached in this essay would demand consideration of the historical theory that there is some peculiarity in our own age really producing an unprecedented cleavage between the Few and the Many, and imposing on popular taste the need of veritable conversion. My own view is that such a situation exists, but that the Highbrow-Lowbrow distinction is one of the things that have helped to produce it. If the people have never shown less taste for good books, it is also true that those capable of writing good books have seldom taken less pains to please the people, or, indeed, so freely insulted them. There are members of the *intelligentsia* at present (some of them socialists) who cannot speak of their cultural inferiors except in accents of passionate hatred and contempt. Certainly it is fatal to approach this or any other quarrel with the assumption that all the faults are on one side: and just as certainly, in all quarrels the task of conciliation belongs *jure divino* to the more reasonable of the two disputants.

VI
THE ALLITERATIVE METRE

'Tis ignorance that makes a barren waste
Of all beyond itself   KEATS

Reprinted from 'Lysist. ata'

THE ALLITERATIVE METRE

IN the general reaction which has set in against the long reign of foreign, syllabic metres in English, it is a little remarkable that few have yet suggested a return to our own ancient system, the alliterative line. Mr. Auden, however, has revived some of its stylistic features; Professor Tolkien will soon, I hope, be ready to publish an alliterative poem; and the moment seems propitious for expounding the principles of this metre to a larger public than those Anglo-Saxon and Old Norse specialists who know it already.

1. Alliteration is no more the whole secret of this verse than rhyme is the whole secret of syllabic verse. It has, in addition, a metrical structure, which could stand alone, and which would then be to this system as blank verse is to the syllabic.

2. Latin verse is based on quantity (= the length of time taken to pronounce a syllable). Modern English is based on stress-accent (= the loudness with which a syllable is pronounced). Alliterative verse involves both.

3. In order to write Alliterative verse it is therefore necessary to learn to distinguish not only accented from unaccented syllables, but also long from short syllables. This is rendered difficult by our classical education which allows boys to pronounce *ille* so that it rhymes with *silly*, and nevertheless to call the first syllable long, which, in their pronunciation, it is not. In dealing with English quantity the reader must learn to attend entirely to *sounds*, and to ignore spelling.

DEFINITION. A long syllable is one which contains *either* a long vowel (as *fath(er)*, *fame, seek, pile, home, do*); *or*, a vowel followed by more than one consonant (as *punt, wind, helm, pelt*).[1]

[Caution. 1. It is here that the trouble from spelling occurs. In modern English spelling, for reasons which need not be discussed here, such words as *silly, pretty, merry, sorrow, attraction*, show a double consonant in spelling where there is no shadow of a double consonant in pronunciation. The reader can convince himself of this by comparing the pretended double T in *pretty* with the real double T in *hot toast*: and he will then hear how a real double consonant renders the first syllable of *hot toast* long, while that of *pretty*, though accented, is short. So, in *distiller* the pretended two L's are one, while in *still life* we have a real double L, disguised as a triple L. True double consonants can be heard in *palely* (cf. *Paley*), *fish-shop* (cf. *bishop*), *unnamed* (cf. *unaimed*), *midday* (cf. *middy*), *solely* (cf. *holy*).[2]

2. In modern English many words, chiefly monosyllables, which end in a single consonant are pronounced differently according to their position in the sentence. If they come at the end of a sentence or other speech-group—that is, if there is a pause after them—the final consonant is so dwelled upon that

[1] That two or more consonants make the *syllable* long is not a metrical rule but a phonetic fact; that they make the preceding *vowel* long, as some say, is neither a rule nor a fact, but false.

[2] -NG in English usually represents a single consonant (G nasalized), but sometimes it represents this consonant followed by a pure G in addition. Hence the first syllable is short in *singer, ringer*: long in *linger, finger*.

the syllable becomes long. If the reader listens carefully he will find that the syllable *man* is short in

> 'Manifold and great mercies'
> or 'The man of property',

but long in

> 'The Invisible Man'
> or 'The Descent of Man'.

With this caution, the reader will be glad to hear, the
serious difficulties in the re-education of our ear are
over.]

4. Each line consists of two half-lines, which are
independent metrical organisms, connected only by
the alliteration.

5. The half-line consists of *Lifts* and *Dips*.

Definitions.

> A Lift = either (*a*) one syllable both long and
> accented (as the first syllable of *ogre, mountain,
> Repton*),
> or (*b*) Two syllables whereof the first is short but
> accented, and the second unaccented (as the
> first *two* syllables of *merrily, vigorous, melancholy,
> evident*).

(Thus in *vary* the first syllable is a Lift: in *very* the
whole word is a Lift.)

> A Dip = any reasonable number of unaccented syl-
> lables whether long or short.

In the following sentences the syllables printed in
Capitals are Lifts, the rest Dips.

> Of COURSE we ASSUME.
> When a phiLOLOGist is a FOOL.
> RhadaMANTHus in his MISERy.

6. Every half-line must contain neither more nor less than two Lifts. (The ancient poetry sometimes introduces a three-lift type which stands to this metre much as the Alexandrine stands to decasyllabics: but the beginner will be wise to neglect it.)

The five different types of half-line depend on the five ways in which Lifts and Dips are combined. Before learning these, however, the reader should 'work his ear in' with the following:

> We were TALKing of DRAGONS, | TOLkien and I
> In a BERKshire BAR. | The BIG WORKman
> Who had SAT SILent | and SUCKED his PIPE
> ALL the EVEning, | from his EMPTY MUG
> with GLEAMing EYE | GLANCED toWARDS us;
> 'I SEEN 'em mySELF', | he SAID FIERCEly.

7. The 'A' type of half-line is arranged Lift-dip, Lift-dip.

> e.g. GREEN and GROWing: MERRY were the MINSTrels: COME from the COUNTry.

Licence. One or two unaccented syllables may be added before the first Lift, forming what is technically known as an Anacrusis.

> e.g. And green and growing: and so merry were the minstrels: he came from the country.

Warning. But this licence should be very seldom used in the second half-line. In the first half-line (i.e. at the beginning of the whole line) it may be used freely.

8. B type = dip-Lift, dip-Lift.

> e.g. and NUMBED with NIGHT: where MAIDS are MERRY: and to the PALACE of PRIDE.

Warning. The first dip may contain 'any reasonable number' of unaccented syllables: but the second should normally consist of a *single* unaccented syllable. In all circumstances a predominantly 'anapaestic' movement is to be avoided.

9. C = dip-Lift, Lift-dip.

(*Note.*—Here we reach a rhythm of daily occurrence in our speech (e.g. 'I can't stand him') which has been allowed no *metrical* recognition for centuries.)

> e.g. The MERRY MASter: In the DARK DUNGeon: Through CLOUDS CLEAving: It is EVER-OPen: And with GOD'S BENISON.

Licence. In this type a *single short, accented* syllable may serve as the second Lift, giving us:

> A cold kipper: but they're hard-headed: a proud palace.

10. D = Lift, Lift-dip.

Here there is only one dip, whereas A, B, and C have two. To compensate for this, in D types the dip must be strengthened by a syllable[1] nearly (but not quite) as strong as the Lifts.

(*Note.*—This again rescues a genuine English speech rhythm from metrical non-existence.)

> e.g. HARD HAYmaking.

It will be heard that the syllable *mak* is as long as, but just less accented than, *hard* and *hay.*

> e.g. BRIGHT QUICKsilver: MAD MERRYmaking: SHODDY SHIPbuilders: GRIM GLADIator: HELL'S HOUSEkeeper.

---

[1] Or, of course, two syllables whereof the first is short. The rules for 'compensating elements' are, in this respect, identical with the rules for Lifts.

In all these examples the strengthening element of the dip stands first in the dip: e.g. in 'Hell's *housekeeper*', *keep-* comes before *-er*. Obviously the reverse order may be used, giving us:

ALL UNDerclothes: MAD MULTitude: EATS ARTichokes: POOR DESTitute.

Licence 1. In D, as in C, a single short, accented syllable may serve as the second Lift, giving us, instead of *Hard haymaking*, such forms as:

SHEER SHOTOVer: PURE PALimpsest.

Licence 2. The compensating element in the dip may also be a single short, accented syllable, giving us:

MAD MELANCHOly: HEAV'N's WAR-office: BORN BOOT-legger.

Licence 3. The sub-type *Mad multitude* may be extended by inserting a single unaccented (and preferably short) syllable between the two Lifts, so as to give:

MAD the MULTitude: EATing ARTichokes.

11. E = Lift-dip-Lift.

Here again we have only one dip, and again the dip must contain a compensating element. E, in fact, is a rearrangement of D.

e.g. HAYmakers HEARD: SHIPbuilders SHOW: GLADiator GRIM.

Licence. The compensating element in the dip may be a single short, accented syllable, giving us:

NEW-College KNOWS.

12. For the reader's convenience, I add a recapitulation of the five types.

A. 1. Green and growing.
   2. (With Anacrusis) The grass is growing.
B.   And life runs low.
C. 1. A dark dungeon.
   2. (With single short for 2nd Lift) The gray gravel.
D. 1. Hell's housekeeper.
   2. (With compensating element last in dip) Earth's antidote.
   3. (With single short for 2nd Lift) East Abingdon.
   4. (With single short for compensating element in dip) Heav'n's war-office.
   5. (Extended) Evil antidote.
E. 1. Shipbuilders show.
   2. (With single short for compensating element in dip) New-College knows.

13. In every line both the Lifts of the first half-line may, and one must, alliterate with the first Lift of the second half-line. As

> In a Berkshire Bar; the Big workman

(both Lifts in the first half alliterating with the first of the second) or,

> We were Talking of dragons, Tolkien and I

(one Lift of the first half alliterating with the first of the second).
An alliteration on all four Lifts as in

> And walks by the waves, as winds warble

is regarded not as an added beauty, but as a deformity. (Its use in Middle English, it will be found, radically alters the character of the metre.)

14. Where only one Lift in the first half-line alliterates, it should normally be the first.

15. All vowels alliterate with one another.
Warning. Do not be deceived by spelling. *Union* alliterates with *yeast, yellow,* &c., not with *uncle.*

16. No half-line of any type should end in a pure dactyl. *Noble Norbury, with trash and trumpery, glancing gloomily,* &c., are unmetrical.

17. *Structure.*
(1) The medial pause which divides the first from the second half of the line must be strictly observed, so that the two halves fall apart as separate speech-groups.

[By speech-groups I mean those units—rhythmical, rhetorical, emotional, and to some extent syntactical, units—out of which our actual conversation is built up. Thus if the reader says 'The big workman who had sat silent and sucked his pipe all the evening', he will (I hope) find that the speech-groups coincide with the half-lines in the example given under para. 6. A good deal of re-education is here necessary, for the chief beauty of syllabic verse lies in a deliberate clash or contradiction between the speech-groups and the 'feet', whereas in alliterative verse the speech-group is both the metrical, and the aesthetic, unit. See below, para. 18.]

> *Examples.* Thus, *he will stand as a stone till the stars crumble,* is metrically good. *The laugh of the lovely lady is silent* is bad. But *Lost is the laugh of the lovely damsel* is not a line at all: for it pretends metrically to be.
> Lost is the laugh of | the lovely damsel

(A-type +A with anacrusis): and in this the first
half is so impossible as a speech-group that a poet
could have written it only because he was really still
thinking in feet and syllables, and not in speech-
groups and half-lines.

(2) But while we cannot run across the medial
break, we can run across the end of a line. In other
words, the last half of a given line and the first half of
the next are more intimately connected than the two
halves of a single line. Hence we may write

> There stands a stone. Still'd is the Lady's
> Peerless laughter.

Corollary. Hence, though the poem begins and ends
with a full line, yet within the poem a new paragraph
or sentence should usually begin in the second half of
a line.

18. *Aesthetics.*

It follows that whereas syllabic poetry primarily uses
the evocative qualities of words (and only secondarily
those of phrases), alliterative poetry reverses the pro-
cedure. The phrase, coinciding with the half-line, is
the poetic unit. In any English country tap-room the
student may hear from the lips of labourers speech-
groups which have a certain race and resonance in
isolation. These are the elements of our native metre.

Such are the rules. Where no tradition—at least
no modern tradition—exists it is rash to offer advice,
but perhaps two counsels may be given. In the first
place, if any one is attracted by the metre in general,
but disposed to omit the rules of quantity and produce
a merely accentual adaptation, I would like to save
him disappointment by warning him that he will

almost certainly produce rubbish. Torture the language, or the thought, as he will, the result will be *thin*. The thing to aim at is richness and fullness of sound, and this cannot be attained without quantity: with quantity, the metre opens possibilities of resonance which have not been exploited for a thousand years. In the second place, I would advise him to be on his guard against too many B types. His iambic training will probably be tempting him to them at every turn: but if he yields his poem will sound like octosyllabics. And lastly, I would advocate to all who have a taste for such things some serious contention with the difficulties of this metre. A few successful specimens would be an excellent answer to the type of critic (by no means extinct) who accuses the moderns of choosing *vers libre* because they are not men enough for metre. For if syllabic verse is like carving in wood and *vers libre* like working with a brush, this is like carving in granite.

A man who preaches a metre must sooner or later risk his case by showing a specimen: and if the fate of Gabriel Harvey deters me, that of Campion invites. In order to avoid misunderstanding I must say that the subject of the following poem was not chosen under the influence of any antiquarian fancy that a medieval metre demanded medieval matter, but because the characters of the planets, as conceived by medieval astrology, seem to me to have a permanent value as spiritual symbols—to provide a *Phänomenologie des Geistes* which is specially worth while in our own generation. Of Saturn we know more than enough. But who does not need to be reminded of Jove?

THE PLANETS

Lady LUNA, in light canoe,	A : B
By friths and shallows of fretted cloudland	B : C
Cruises monthly; with chrism of dews	A : B
And drench of dream, a drizzling glamour,	B : B
Enchants us—the cheat! changing sometime	B : A
A mind to madness, melancholy pale,	A 2 : E 2
Bleached with gazing on her blank count'nance	A : C
Orb'd and ageless. In earth's bosom	A : C 2
The shower of her rays, sharp-feathered light	B : E 2
Reaching downward, ripens silver,	A : A
Forming and fashioning female brightness,	A : A
—Metal maidenlike. Her moist circle	D 2 : C
Is nearest earth. Next beyond her	B : A
MERCURY marches;—madcap rover,	A : A
Patron of pilf'rers. Pert quicksilver	A : D
His gaze begets, goblin mineral,	B : A
Merry multitude of meeting selves,	D 2 : B
Same but sundered. From the soul's darkness,	A : C
With wreathèd wand,[1] words he marshals,	B : A
Guides and gathers them—gay bellwether	A : D 4
Of flocking fancies. His flint has struck	C : B
The spark of speech from spirit's tinder,	B : C
Lord of language! He leads forever	A : B
The spangle and splendour, sport that mingles	A 2 : A
Sound with senses, in subtle pattern,	A : C 2
Words in wedlock, and wedding also	A : C
Of thing with thought. In the third region	B : C
VENUS voyages . . . but my voice falters;	A : C
Rude rime-making wrongs her beauty,	D : A
Whose breasts and brow, and her breath's sweet- ness	B : C
Bewitch the worlds. Wide-spread the reign	B : E
Of her secret sceptre, in the sea's caverns,	A 2 : C 2

[1] Alliteration on second lift of the first half. The orthographic w in *wreathèd* has, of course, no metrical function.

K

In grass growing, and grain bursting,	C : C
Flower unfolding, and flesh longing,	A : C
And shower falling sharp in April.	C : A
The metal of copper in the mine reddens	B : C 2
With muffled brightness, like muted gold,	C : B
By her finger form'd. Far beyond her	B : A
The heaven's highway hums and trembles,	C : A
Drums and dindles,[1] to the driv'n thunder	A : C
Of SOL's chariot, whose sword of light	C : B
Hurts and humbles; beheld only	A : C
Of eagle's eye. When his arrow glances	B : C
Through mortal mind, mists are parted	B : A
And mild as morning the mellow wisdom	A 2 : C
Breathes o'er the breast, broadening eastward	E : A
Clear and cloudless. In a clos'd garden	A : C
(Unbound her burden) his beams foster	A 2 : C
Soul in secret, where the soil puts forth	A : B
Paradisal palm, and pure fountains	E : C
Turn and re-temper, touching coolly	A : A
The uncomely common to cordial gold;	B : B
Whose ore also, in earth's matrix,	C : C
Is print and pressure of his proud signet	B : C
On the wax of the world. He is the worshipp'd	
male,	B : B
The earth's husband, all-beholding,	C : A
Arch-chemic eye. But other country	E 2 : C
Dark with discord dins beyond him,	A : A
With noise of nakers, neighing of horses,	B : A
Hammering of harness. A haughty god	A : B
MARS mercenary,[2] makes there his camp	D 2 : E
And flies his flag; flaunts laughingly	B : D
The graceless beauty, grey-eyed and keen,	A 2 : E
—Blond insolence—of his blithe visage	D 2 : C 2
Which is hard and happy. He hews the act,	B : B

[1] Cf. Malory, v, cap. 8.
[2] -ARY being the compensating element in the Dip.

The indifferent deed with dint of his mallet	B : B
And his chisel of choice; achievement comes not	B : A 2
Unhelped by him;—hired gladiator	B : D
Of evil and good. All's one to Mars,	B : E
The wrong righted, rescued meekness,	C : A
Or trouble in trenches, with trees splintered	A : C
And birds banished, banks fill'd with gold	C 2 : E
And the liar made lord. Like handiwork	B : D 2
He offers to all—earns his wages	B : A
And whistles the while. White-featured dread	B : E
Mars has mastered. His metal's iron	A : C
That was hammered through hands into holy cross,	B : B
Cruel carpentry. He is cold and strong,	D 5 : B
Necessity's son.[1] Soft breathes the air	B : E
Mild, and meadowy, as we mount further	A : C
Where rippled radiance rolls about us	C : A
Moved with music—measureless the waves'	A : E
Joy and jubilee. It is JOVE's orbit,	D 5 : C
Filled and festal, faster turning	A : A
With arc ampler. From the Isles of Tin	C : B
Tyrian traders, in trouble steering	A : C
Came with his cargoes; the Cornish treasure	A : B
That his ray ripens. Of wrath ended	C : C
And woes mended, of winter passed	C : B
And guilt forgiven, and good fortune	B : C
Jove is master; and of jocund revel,	A : C 2
Laughter of ladies. The lion-hearted,	A : A 2
The myriad-minded, men like the gods,	A 2 : E
Helps and heroes, helms of nations	A : A
Just and gentle, are Jove's children,	A : C
Work his wonders. On his wide forehead[2]	A : C 2

[1] The c in *necessity*, being an s in pronunciation, carries the first alliteration.

[2] This is c 2 in my pronunciation because I pronounce *forehead* so as to rhyme with *horrid*. In the alternative pronunciation (which is now heard even among educated speakers) it would be c 1.

Calm and kingly, no care darkens	A : C
Nor wrath wrinkles: but righteous power	C : B
And leisure and largess their loose splendours	A 2 : C
Have wrapped around him—a rich mantle	A 2 : C
Of ease and empire. Up far beyond	A 2 : E
Goes SATURN silent in the seventh region,	C : C
The skirts of the sky. Scant grows the light,	B : E
Sickly, uncertain (the Sun's finger	A : C
Daunted with darkness). Distance hurts us,	A : A
And the vault severe of vast silence;	B : C
Where fancy fails us, and fair language,	A 2 : C
And love leaves us, and light fails us	C : C
And Mars fails us, and the mirth of Jove	C : B
Is as tin tinkling. In tattered garment,	C : C
Weak with winters, he walks forever	A : B
A weary way, wide round the heav'n,	B : E
Stoop'd and stumbling, with staff groping,	A : C
The lord of lead. He is the last planet	B : C 2
Old and ugly. His eye fathers	A : C
Pale pestilence, pain of envy,	D 2 : A
Remorse and murder. Melancholy drink	A : E 2
(For bane or blessing) of bitter wisdom	B : C
He pours for his people, a perilous draught	A 2 : B
That the lip loves not. We leave all things	C : C
To reach the rim of the round welkin,	B : C
Heaven's hermitage, high and lonely.	D 2 : A

VII

BLUSPELS AND FLALANSFERES: A SEMANTIC NIGHTMARE

We are often compelled to set up standards we cannot reach
ourselves and to lay down rules we could not ourselves
satisfy.

LORD COLERIDGE, C.J. (Law Reports, Queen's Bench Division XIV, p. 288 in *Reg.* v. *Dudley and Stephens*).

Read at Manchester University

PHILOLOGISTS often tell us that our language is full of dead metaphors. In this sentence, the word 'dead' and the word 'metaphors' may turn out to be ambiguous; but the fact, or group of facts, referred to, is one about which there is no great disagreement. We all know in a rough and ready way, and all admit, these things which are being called 'dead metaphors', and for the moment I do not propose to debate the propriety of the name. But while their existence is not disputed, their nature, and their relation to thought, gives rise to a great deal of controversy. For the benefit of any who happen to have avoided this controversy hitherto, I had better make plain what it is, by a concrete example. Bréal in his *Semantics* often spoke in metaphorical, that is consciously, rhetorically, metaphorical language, of language itself. Messrs. Ogden and Richards in *The Meaning of Meaning* took Bréal to task on the ground that 'it is impossible thus to handle a scientific subject in metaphorical terms'. Barfield in his *Poetic Diction* retorted that Ogden and Richards were, as a matter of fact, just as metaphorical as Bréal. They had forgotten, he complained, that all language has a figurative origin and that the 'scientific' terms on which they piqued themselves—words like *organism, stimulus, reference*—were not miraculously exempt. On the contrary, he maintained, 'these authors who professed to eschew figurative expressions were really confining themselves to one very old kind of figure; they were rigid under the spell of those verbal ghosts

of the physical sciences which to-day make up practi-
cally the whole meaning-system of so many European
minds'.[1] Whether Ogden and Richards will see fit,
or have seen fit, to reply to this, I do not know; but
the lines on which any reply would run are already
traditional. In fact the whole debate may be represented by a very simple dialogue.

A. You are being metaphorical.

B. You are just as metaphorical as I am, but you
don't know it.

A. No, I'm not. Of course I know all about *attend-
ing* once having meant *stretching*, and the rest of it.
But that is not what it means now. It may have been
a metaphor to Adam—but I am not using it metaphorically. What I *mean* is a pure concept with no
metaphor about it at all. The fact that it *was* a metaphor is no more relevant than the fact that my pen is
made of wood. You are simply confusing derivation
with meaning.

There is clearly a great deal to be said for both
sides. On the one hand it seems odd to suppose that
what we *mean* is conditioned by a dead metaphor of
which we may be quite ignorant. On the other hand,
we see from day to day, that when a man uses a
current and admitted metaphor without knowing it,
he usually gets led into nonsense; and when, we are
tempted to ask, does a metaphor become so old that
we can ignore it with impunity? It seems harsh to
rule that a man must know the whole semantic history
of every word he uses—a history usually undiscover-
able—or else talk without thinking. And yet, on the

[1] A. O. Barfield, *Poetic Diction*, 1928, pp. 139, 140.

other hand, an obstinate suspicion creeps in that we cannot entirely jump off our own shadows, and that we deceive ourselves if we suppose that a new and purely conceptual notion of *attention* has replaced and superseded the old metaphor of stretching. Here, then, is the problem which I want to consider. How far, if at all, is thinking limited by these dead metaphors? Is Anatole France in any sense right when he reduces 'The soul possesses God' to 'the breath sits on the bright sky?' Or is the other party right when it urges 'Derivations are one thing. Meanings are another'? Or is the truth somewhere between them?

The first and easiest case to study is that in which we ourselves invent a new metaphor. This may happen in one of two ways. It may be that when we are trying to express clearly to ourselves or to others a conception which we have never perfectly understood, a new metaphor simply starts forth, under the pressure of composition or argument. When this happens, the result is often as surprising and illuminating to us as to our audience; and I am inclined to think that this is what happens with the great, new metaphors of the poets. And when it does happen, it is plain that our new understanding is bound up with the new metaphor. In fact, the situation is for our purpose indistinguishable from that which arises when we hear a new metaphor from others; and for that reason, it need not be separately discussed. One of the ways, then, in which we invent a new metaphor, is by *finding* it, as unexpectedly as we might find it in the pages of a book; and whatever is true of the new metaphors that we find in books will also be true of those which we reach by a kind of lucky chance, or inspiration. But, of course, there is another way in which we invent new metaphors. When we are trying to explain, to some one younger or less instructed than ourselves, a matter which is already perfectly clear in our own minds, we may deliberately, and even painfully, pitch about for the metaphor that is likely to help him. Now when this happens, it is quite plain that our thought, our power of meaning, is not much helped or hindered by the metaphor that we use. On the contrary, we are often acutely aware of the discrepancy between our meaning and our image. We know that our metaphor is in some respects misleading; and probably, if we have acquired the tutorial shuffle, we warn our audience that it is 'not to be pressed'. It is apparently possible, in this case at least, to use metaphor and yet to keep our thinking independent of it. But we must observe that it is possible, only because we have other methods of expressing the same idea. We have already our own way of expressing the thing: we could say it, or we suppose that we could say it, literally instead. This clear conception we owe to other sources—to our previous studies. We can adopt the new metaphor as a temporary tool which we dominate and by which we are not dominated ourselves, only because we have other tools in our box.

Let us now take the opposite situation—that in which it is we ourselves who are being instructed. I am no mathematician; and some one is trying to explain to me the theory that space is finite. Stated

thus, the new doctrine is, to me, meaningless. But
suppose he proceeds as follows.

'You,' he may say, 'can intuit only three dimensions; you therefore cannot conceive how space should
be limited. But I think I can show you how that
which must appear infinite in three dimensions,
might nevertheless be finite in four. Look at it this
way. Imagine a race of people who knew only two
dimensions—like the Flatlanders. And suppose they
were living on a globe. They would have no conception, of course, that the globe was curved—for it is
curved round in that third dimension of which they
have no inkling. They will therefore imagine that
they are living on a plane; but they will soon find
out that it is a plane which nowhere comes to an end;
there are no edges to it. Nor would they be able
even to imagine an edge. For an edge would mean
that, after a certain point, there would be nothing to
walk on; nothing below their feet. But that *below*
and *above* dimension is just what their minds have
not got; they have only backwards and forwards, and
left and right. They would thus be forced to assert
that their globe, which they could not see as a globe,
was infinite. You can see perfectly well that it is
finite. And now, can you not conceive that as these
Flatlanders are to you, so you might be to a creature
that intuited four dimensions? Can you not conceive how that which seems necessarily infinite to
your three-dimensional consciousness might none
the less be really finite?' The result of such a metaphor on my mind would be—in fact, has been—that
something which before was sheerly meaningless

acquires at least a faint hint of meaning. And if the particular example does not appeal to every one, yet every one has had experiences of the same sort. For all of us there are things which we cannot fully understand at all, but of which we can get a faint inkling by means of metaphor. And in such cases the relation between the thought and the metaphor is precisely the opposite of the relation which arises when it is we ourselves who understand and then invent the metaphors to help others. We are here entirely at the mercy of the metaphor. If our instructor has chosen it badly, we shall be thinking nonsense. If we have not got the imagery clearly before us, we shall be thinking nonsense. If we have it before us without knowing that it is metaphor—if we forget that our Flatlanders on their globe are a copy of the thing and mistake them for the thing itself—then again we shall be thinking nonsense. What truth we can attain in such a situation depends rigidly on three conditions. First, that the imagery should be originally well chosen; secondly, that we should apprehend the exact imagery; and thirdly that we should know that the metaphor is a metaphor. (That metaphors, misread as statements of fact, are the source of monstrous errors, need hardly be pointed out.)

I have now attempted to show two different kinds of metaphorical situation as they are at their birth. They are the two extremes, and furnish the limits within which our inquiry must work. On the one hand, there is the metaphor which we invent to teach by; on the other, the metaphor from which we learn. They might be called the Master's metaphor, and the Pupil's metaphor. The first is freely chosen; it is one among many possible modes of expression; it does not at all hinder, and only very slightly helps, the thought of its maker. The second is not chosen at all; it is the unique expression of a meaning that we cannot have on any other terms; it dominates completely the thought of the recipient; his truth cannot rise above the truth of the original metaphor. And between the Master's metaphor and the Pupil's there comes, of course, an endless number of types, dotted about in every kind of intermediate position. Indeed, these Pupil-Teachers' metaphors are the ordinary stuff of our conversation. To divide them into a series of classes and sub-classes and to attempt to discuss these separately would be very laborious, and, I trust, unnecessary. If we can find a true doctrine about the two extremes, we shall not be at a loss to give an account of what falls between them. To find the truth about any given metaphorical situation will merely be to plot its position. In so far as it inclines to the 'magistral' extreme, so far our thought will be independent of it; in so far as it has a 'pupillary' element, so far it will be the unique expression, and therefore the iron limit of our thinking. To fill in this framework would be, as Aristotle used to say, 'anybody's business'.

Our problem, it will be remembered, was the problem of 'dead' or 'forgotten' metaphors. We have now gained some light on the relation between thought and metaphor as it is at the outset, when the metaphor is first made; and we have seen that this relation varies greatly according to what I have called the 'metaphorical situation'. There is, in fact, one relation in the case of the Master's metaphor, and an almost opposite relation in that of the Pupil's metaphor. The next step must clearly be to see what becomes of these two relations as the metaphors in question progress to the state of death or fossilization.

The question of the Master's Metaphor need not detain us long. I may attempt to explain the Kantian philosophy to a pupil by the following metaphor. 'Kant answered the question "How do I know that whatever comes round the corner will be blue?" by the supposition "I am wearing blue spectacles." In time I may come to use "the blue spectacles" as a kind of shorthand for the whole Kantian machinery of the categories and forms of perception. And let us suppose, for the sake of analogy with the real history of language, that I continue to use this expression long after I have forgotten the metaphor which originally gave rise to it. And perhaps by this time the form of the word will have changed. Instead of the 'blue spectacles' I may now talk of the *bloospel* or even the *bluspel*. If I live long enough to reach my dotage I may even enter on a philological period in which I attempt to find the derivation of this mysterious word. I may suppose that the second element is derived from the word *spell* and look back with interest on the supposed period when Kant appeared to me to be magical; or else, arguing that the whole word is clearly formed on the analogy of *gospel*, may indulge in unhistorical reminiscences of the days when the *Critique* seemed to me irrefragably

true. But how far, if at all, will my thinking about
Kant be affected by all this linguistic process? In
practice, no doubt, there will be some subtle influence; the mere continued use of the word *bluspel*
may have led me to attribute to it a unity and sub-
stantiality which I should have hesitated to attribute
to 'the whole Kantian machinery of the categories
and forms of perception'. But that is a result rather
of the noun-making than of the death of the metaphor. It is an interesting fact, but hardly relevant to
our present inquiry. For the rest, the mere forgetting
of the metaphor does not seem to alter my thinking
about Kant, just as the original metaphor did not
limit my thinking about Kant; provided always—
and this is of the last importance—that it was, to
begin with, a genuine Master's metaphor. I had my
conception of Kant's philosophy before I ever thought
of the blue spectacles. If I have continued philosophical studies I have it still. The 'blue spectacles'
phrase was from the first a temporary dress assumed
by my thought for a special purpose, and ready to be
laid aside at my pleasure; it did not penetrate the
thinking itself, and its subsequent history is irrelevant.
To any one who attempts to refute my later views on
Kant by telling me that I don't know the real meaning of *bluspel*, I may confidently retort 'Derivations
aren't meanings'. To be sure, if there was any *pupillary* element in its original use, if I received, as well
as gave, new understanding when I used it, then the
whole situation will be different. And it is fair to
admit that in practice very few metaphors can be
purely magistral; only that which to some degree

enlightens ourselves is likely to enlighten others. It is hardly possible that when I first used the metaphor of the blue spectacles I did not gain some new awareness of the Kantian philosophy; and, so far, it was not purely magistral. But I am deliberately idealizing for the sake of clarity. Purely magistral metaphor may never occur. What is important for us is to grasp that *just in so far* as any metaphor began by being magistral, so far I can continue to use it long after I have forgotten its metaphorical nature, and my thinking will be neither helped nor hindered by the fact that it was originally a metaphor, nor yet by my forgetfulness of that fact. It is a mere accident. Here, derivations are irrelevant to meanings.

Let us now turn to the opposite situation, that of the Pupil's Metaphor. And let us continue to use our old example of the unmathematical man who has had the finitude of space suggested to him (we can hardly say 'explained') by the metaphor of the Flatlanders on their sphere. The question here is rather more complicated. In the case of the Master's metaphor, by hypothesis, the master knew, and would continue to know, what he meant, independently of the metaphor. In the present instance, however, the fossilization of the metaphor may take place in two different ways. The pupil may himself become a mathematician, or he may remain as ignorant of mathematics as he was before; and in either case, he may continue to use the metaphor of the Flatlanders while forgetting its real content and its metaphorical nature.

I will take the second possibility first. From the imagery of the Flatlanders' sphere I have got my first inkling of the new meaning. My thought is entirely conditioned by this imagery. I do not apprehend the thing at all, except by seeing 'it could be something like this'. Let us suppose that in my anxiety to docket this new experience, I label the inkling or vague notion, 'the Flatlanders' sphere'. When I next hear the fourth dimension spoken of, I shall say, 'Ah yes—the Flatlanders' sphere and all that'. In a few years (to continue our artificial parallel) I may be talking glibly of the *Flalansfere* and may even have forgotten the whole of the imagery which this word once represented. And I am still, according to the hypothesis, profoundly ignorant of mathematics. My situation will then surely be most ridiculous. The meaning of *Flalansfere* I never knew except through the imagery. I could get beyond the imagery, to that whereof the imagery was a copy, only by learning mathematics; but this I have neglected to do. Yet I have lost the imagery. Nothing remains, then, but the conclusion that the word *Flalansfere* is now really meaningless. My thinking, which could never get beyond the imagery, at once its boundary and its support, has now lost that support. I mean strictly nothing when I speak of the *Flalansfere*. I am only talking, not thinking, when I use the word. But this fact will be long concealed from me, because *Flalansfere*, being a noun, can be endlessly fitted into various contexts, so as to conform to syntactical usage and to give an appearance of meaning. It will even conform to the logical rules; and I can make many judgements about the *Flalansfere*; such as *it is what it is*, and has *attributes* (for otherwise of course it wouldn't be a thing, and if it wasn't a thing, how could I be talking about it?), and is a *substance* (for it can be the subject of a sentence). And what *affective* overtones the word may have taken on by that time, it is dangerous to predict. It had an air of mystery from the first: before the end I shall probably be building temples to it, and exhorting my countrymen to fight and die for the *Flalansfere*. But the *Flalansfere*, when once we have forgotten the metaphor, is only a noise.

But how if I proceed, after once having grasped the metaphor of the Flatlanders, to become a mathematician? In this case, too, I may well continue to use the metaphor, and may corrupt it in form till it becomes a single noun, the *Flalansfere*. But I shall have advanced, by other means, from the original symbolism; and I shall be able to study the thing symbolized without reference to the metaphor that first introduced me to it. It will then be no harm though I should forget that *Flalansfere* had ever been metaphorical. As the metaphor, even if it survived, would no longer limit my thoughts, so its fossilization cannot confuse them.

The results which emerge may now be summarized as follows. Our thought is independent of the metaphors we employ, in so far as these metaphors are optional: that is, in so far as we are able to have the same idea without them. For that is the real characteristic both of the magistral metaphors and of those which become optional, as the Flatlanders would become, if the pupil learned mathematics. On the other hand, where the metaphor is our only method of reaching a given idea at all, there our thinking is limited by the metaphor so long as we retain the metaphor; and when the metaphor becomes fossilized, our 'thinking' is not thinking at all, but mere sound or mere incipient movements in the larynx. We are now in a position to reply to the statement that 'Derivations are not meanings', and to the claim that 'we know what we mean by words without knowing the fossilized metaphors they contain'. We can see that such a statement, as it stands, is neither wholly true nor wholly false. The truth will vary from word to word, and from speaker to speaker. No rule of thumb is possible, we must take every case on its merits. A word can bear a meaning in the mouth of a speaker who has forgotten its hidden metaphor, and a meaning independent of that metaphor, but only on certain conditions. Either the metaphor must have been optional from the beginning, and have remained optional through all the generations of its use, so that the conception has always used and still uses the imagery as a mere tool; or else, at some period subsequent to its creation, we must have gone on to acquire, independently of the metaphor, such new knowledge of the object indicated by it as enables us now, at least, to dispense with it. To put the same thing in another way, meaning is independent of derivation, only if the metaphor was originally 'magistral'; or if, in the case of an originally pupillary metaphor, some quite new kind of apprehension has arisen to replace the metaphorical apprehension which has been lost. The two conditions may be best illustrated by a concrete example. Let us take the word for *soul* as it exists in the Romance language. How far is a man entitled to say that what he means by the word *âme* or *anima* is quite independent of the image of *breathing*, and that he means just the same (and just as much) whether he happens to know that 'derivation' or not? We can only answer that it depends on a variety of things. I will enumerate all the formal possibilities for the sake of clearness: one of them, of course, is too grotesque to appear for any other purpose.

1. The metaphor may originally have been magistral. Primitive men, we are to suppose, were clearly aware, on the one hand, of an entity called *soul*; and, on the other, of a process or object called *breath*. And they used the second figuratively to suggest the first—presumably when revealing their wisdom to primitive women and primitive children. And we may suppose, further, that this magistral relation to the metaphor has never been lost: that all generations, from the probably arboreal to the man saying 'Blast your soul' in a pub this evening, have kept clearly before them these two separate entities, and used the one metaphorically to denote the other, while at the same time being well able to conceive the soul unmetaphorically, and using the metaphor merely as a colour or trope which adorned but did not influence their thought. Now if all this were true, it would unquestionably follow that when a man says *anima* his meaning is not affected by the old image of breath; and also, it does not matter in the least whether he knows that the word once sug-

gested that image or not. But of course all this is
not true.

2. The metaphor may originally have been pupillary. So far from being a voluntary ornament or
paedagogic device, the ideas of *breath* or *something like
breath* may have been the only possible inkling that
our parents could gain of the soul. But if this was so,
how does the modern user of the word stand?
Clearly, if he has ceased to be aware of the metaphorical element in *anima*, without replacing the metaphorical apprehension by some new knowledge of
the soul, borrowed from other sources, then he will
mean nothing by it; we must not, on that account,
suppose that he will cease to use it, or even to use it
(as we say) intelligibly—i.e. to use it in sentences
constructed according to the laws of grammar, and
to insert these sentences into those conversational and
literary contexts where usage demands their inser-
tion. If, on the other hand, he has some independent
knowledge of the entity which our ancestors indicated by their metaphor of breath, then indeed he
may mean something.

I take it that it is this last situation in which we
commonly suppose ourselves to be. It doesn't matter,
we would claim, what the majestic root GNA really
stood for: we have learned a great deal about *knowing*
since those days, and it is these more recent acquisitions that we use in our thinking. The first name for
a thing may easily be determined by some incon-
siderable accident. As we learn more, we mean

more; the radical meaning of the old syllables does not bind us; what we have learned since has set us free. Assuredly, the accident which led the Romans to call all Hellenes *Graeci* did not continue to limit their power of apprehending Greece. And as long as we are dealing with sensible objects this view is hardly to be disputed. The difficulty begins with objects of thought. It may be stated as follows.

Our claim to independence of the metaphor is, as we have seen, a claim to know the object otherwise than through that metaphor. If we can throw the Flatlanders overboard and still think the fourth dimension, then, and not otherwise, we can forget what *Flalansfere* once meant and still think coherently. That was what happened, you will remember, to the man who went on and learned mathematics. He came to apprehend that of which the Flatlanders' sphere was only the image, and consequently was free to think beyond the metaphor and to forget the metaphor altogether. In our previous account of him, however, we carefully omitted to draw attention to one very remarkable fact: namely, that when he deserted metaphor for mathematics, he did not really pass from symbol to symbolized, but only from one set of symbols to another. The equations and what-nots are as unreal, as metaphorical, if you like, as the Flatlanders' sphere. The mathematical problem I need not pursue further; we see at once that it casts a disquieting light on our linguistic problem. We have hitherto been speaking as if we had two methods of thought open to us: the metaphorical, and the literal. We talked as if the creator of a magistral

metaphor had it always in his power to think the
same concept *literally* if he chose. We talked as if the
present-day user of the word *anima* could prove his
right to neglect that word's buried metaphor by
turning round and giving us an account of the soul
which was not metaphorical at all. That he has
power to dispense with the particular metaphor of
breath, is of course agreed. But we have not yet
inquirèd what he can substitute for it. If we turn to
those who are most anxious to tell us about the soul—
I mean the psychologists—we shall find that the
word *anima* has simply been replaced by complexes,
repressions, censors, engrams, and the like. In other
words the *breath* has been exchanged for *tyings-up*,
shovings-back, *Roman magistrates*, and *scratchings*. If we
inquire what has replaced the metaphorical *bright
sky* of primitive theology, we shall only get a *perfect
substance*, that is, a *completely made lying-under*, or—
which is very much better, but equally metaphorical—a universal Father, or perhaps (in English) a
loaf-carver, in Latin a *householder*, in Romance *a person
older than*. The point need not be laboured. It is
abundantly clear that the freedom from a given
metaphor which we admittedly enjoy in some cases
is often only a freedom to choose between that metaphor and others.

Certain reassurances may, indeed, be held out. In
the first place, our distinction between the different
kinds of metaphorical situation can stand; though it
is hardly so important as we had hoped. To have a
choice of metaphors (as we have in some cases) is to
know more than we know when we are the slaves of

a unique metaphor. And, in the second place, all description or identification, all direction of our own thought or another's, is not so metaphorical as definition. If, when challenged on the word *anima*, we proceed to define, we shall only reshuffle the buried metaphors; but if we simply say (or think) 'what I am', or 'what is going on in here', we shall have at least something before us which we do not know by metaphor. We shall at least be no worse off than the arboreal psychologists. At the same time, this method will not really carry us far. 'What's going on here' is really the content of *haec anima*: for *anima* we want '*The sort of thing* that is going on here', and once we are committed to *sorts* and *kinds* we are adrift among metaphors.

We have already said that when a man claims to think independently of the buried metaphor in one of his words, his claim may sometimes be allowed. But it was allowed only in so far as he could really supply the place of that buried metaphor with new and independent apprehension of his own. We now see that this new apprehension will usually turn out to be itself metaphorical; or else, what is very much worse, instead of new apprehension we shall have simply words—each word enshrining one more ignored metaphor. For if he does not know the history of *anima*, how should he know the history of the equally metaphorical words in which he defines it, if challenged? And if he does not know their history and therefore their metaphors, and if he cannot define *them* without yet further metaphors, what can his discourse be but an endless ringing of the changes on

such *bluspels* and *Flalansferes* as seem to mean, indeed,
but do not mean? In reality, the man has played us
a very elementary trick. He claimed that he could
think without metaphor, and in ignorance of the
metaphors fossilized in his words. He made good the
claim by pointing to the knowledge of his object
which he possessed independently of the metaphor;
and the proof of this knowledge was the definition or
description which he could produce. We did not at
first observe that where we were promised a freedom
from metaphor we were given only a power of
changing the metaphors in rapid succession. The
things he speaks of he has never apprehended
literally. Yet only such genuinely literal apprehension could enable him to forget the metaphors
which he was actually using and yet to have a
meaning. Either literalness, or else metaphor understood: one or other of these we must have; the third
alternative is nonsense. But literalness we cannot
have. The man who does not consciously use metaphors talks without meaning. We might even formu-
late a rule: the meaning in any given composition is
in inverse ratio to the author's belief in his own
literalness.

If a man has seen ships and the sea, he may abandon
the metaphor of a *sea-stallion* and call a boat a boat.
But suppose a man who has never seen the sea, or
ships, yet who knows of them just as much as he can
glean, say from the following list of *Kenningar*—sea-
stallions, winged logs, wave riders, ocean trains. If
he keeps all these together in his mind, and knows
them for the metaphors they are, he will be able to

think of ships, very imperfectly indeed, and under strict limits, but not wholly in vain. But if instead of this he pins his faith on the particular *kenning ocean-trains*, because that *kenning*, with its comfortable air of machinery, seems to him somehow more safely prosaic, less flighty and dangerous than its fellows, and if, contracting that to the form *oshtrans*, he proceeds to forget that it was a metaphor, then, while he talks grammatically, he has ceased to think of anything. It will not avail him to stamp his feet and swear that he is literal; to say 'An *oshtran* is an *oshtran*, and there's an end. I mean what I mean. What I mean is what I say.'

The remedy lies, indeed, in the opposite direction. When we pass beyond pointing to individual sensible objects, when we begin to think of causes, relations, of mental states or acts, we become incurably metaphorical. We apprehend none of these things except through metaphor: we know of the ships only what the *Kenningar* will tell us. Our only choice is to use the metaphors and thus to think something, though less than we could wish; or else to be driven by unrecognized metaphors and so think nothing at all. I myself would prefer to embrace the former choice, as far as my ignorance and laziness allow me.

To speak more plainly, he who would increase the meaning and decrease the meaningless verbiage in his own speech and writing, must do two things. He must become conscious of the fossilized metaphors in his words; and he must freely use new metaphors, which he creates for himself. The first depends upon knowledge, and therefore on leisure; the second on a certain degree of imaginative ability. The second is perhaps the more important of the two: we are never less the slaves of metaphor than when we are making metaphor, or hearing it new made. When we are thinking hard of the Flatlanders, and at the same time fully aware that they *are* a metaphor, we are in a situation almost infinitely superior to that of the man who talks of the *Flalansfere* and thinks that he is being literal and straightforward.

If our argument has been sound, it leads us to certain rather remarkable conclusions. In the first place it would seem that we must be content with a very modest quantity of thinking as the core of all our talking. I do not wish to exaggerate our poverty. Not all our words are equally metaphorical, not all our metaphors are equally forgotten. And even where the old metaphor is lost there is often a hope that we may still restore meaning by pointing to some sensible object, some sensation, or some concrete memory. But no man can or will confine his cognitive efforts to this narrow field. At the very humblest we must speak of things in the plural; we must point not only to isolated sensations, but to groups and classes of sensations; and the universal latent in every group and every plural inflection cannot be thought without metaphor. Thus far beyond the security of literal meaning all of us, we may be sure, are going to be driven by our daily needs; indeed, not to go thus far would be to abandon reason itself. In practice we all really intend to go much farther. Why should we not? We have in our hands the key of metaphor, and it would be

pusillanimous to abandon its significant use, because
we have come to realize that its meaningless use is
necessarily prevalent. We must indeed learn to use
it more cautiously; and one of the chief benefits to
be derived from our inquiry is the new standard of
criticism which we must henceforward apply both to
our own apparent thought and to that of others.
We shall find, too, that real meaning, judged by
this standard, does not come always where we have
learned to expect. *Flalansferes* and *bluspels* will clearly
be most prevalent in certain types of writers. The
percentage of mere syntax masquerading as meaning
may vary from something like 100 per cent. in political
writers, journalists, psychologists, and economists, to
something like forty per cent. in the writers of children's stories. Some scientists will fare better than
others: the historian, the geographer, and sometimes
the biologist will speak significantly more often than
their colleagues; the mathematician, who seldom for-
gets that his symbols are symbolic, may often rise for
short stretches to ninety per cent. of meaning and ten
of verbiage. The philosophers will differ as widely
from one another as any of the other groups differ
among themselves: for a good metaphysical library
contains at once some of the most verbal, and some
of the most significant literature in the world. Those
who have prided themselves on being literal, and
who have endeavoured to speak plainly, with no mystical tomfoolery, about the highest abstractions, will
be found to be among the least significant of writers:
I doubt if we shall find more than a beggarly five
per cent. of meaning in the pages of some celebrated

'tough minded' thinkers, and how the account of
Kant or Spinoza stands, none knows but heaven.
But open your Plato, and you will find yourself
among the great creators of metaphor, and therefore among the masters of meaning. If we turn to
Theology—or rather to the literature of religion—
the result will be more surprising still; for unless
our whole argument is wrong, we shall have to
admit that a man who says *heaven* and thinks of
the visible sky is pretty sure to mean more than
a man who tells us that heaven is a state of mind.
It may indeed be otherwise; the second man may
be a mystic who is remembering and pointing to
an actual and concrete experience of his own. But
it is long, long odds. Bunyan and Dante stand
where they did; the scale of Bishop Butler, and of
better men than he, flies up and kicks the beam.

It will have escaped no one that in such a scale of
writers the poets will take the highest place; and
among the poets those who have at once the tenderest
care for old words and the surest instinct for the
creation of new metaphors. But it must not be
supposed that I am in any sense putting forward
the imagination as the organ of truth. We are not
talking of truth, but of meaning: meaning which is
the antecedent condition both of truth and false-
hood, whose antithesis is not error but nonsense.
I am a rationalist. For me, reason is the natural
organ of truth; but imagination is the organ of
meaning. Imagination, producing new metaphors
or revivifying old, is not the cause of truth, but its
condition. It is, I confess, undeniable that such a

view indirectly implies a kind of truth or rightness in the imagination itself. I said at the outset that the truth we won by metaphor could not be greater than the truth of the metaphor itself; and we have seen since that all our truth, or all but a few fragments, is won by metaphor. And thence, I confess, it does follow that if our thinking is ever true, then the metaphors by which we think must have been good metaphors. It does follow that if those original equations, between good and light, or evil and dark, between breath and soul and all the others, were from the beginning arbitrary and fanciful—if there is not, in fact, a kind of psycho-physical parallelism (or more) in the universe—then all our thinking is nonsensical. But we cannot, without contradiction, believe it to be nonsensical. And so, admittedly, the view I have taken has metaphysical implications. But so has every view.

VIII

VARIATION IN SHAKESPEARE
AND OTHERS

Sententia cum sit
Unica, non uno veniat contenta paratu,
Sed variet vestes et mutatoria sumat.
Sub verbis aliis praesumpta resume, repone
Pluribus in clausis unum; multiplice forma
Dissimuletur idem; varius sis et tamen idem.

GEFFROI DE VINSAUF, *Poetria Nova*, pp. 220 *et seq.*

Read to the Mermaid Club

VARIATION IN SHAKESPEARE AND OTHERS

ONE day[1] in March, 1781, Mrs. Thrale and Boswell presented the Doctor with a problem. Had Shakespeare or Milton drawn the more admirable picture of a man? The passages produced on either side were Hamlet's description of his father, and Milton's description of Adam. They run as follows.

> See what a grace was seated on this brow,
> Hyperion's curls, the front of Jove himself,
> An eye like Mars, to threaten and command,
> A station like the herald Mercury
> New lighted on a heaven kissing hill;
> A combination and a form, indeed,
> Where every God did seem to set his seal
> To give the world assurance of a man.

> His fair large front and eye sublime declar'd
> Absolute rule: and hyacinthine locks
> Round from his parted forelock manly hung
> Clustering, but not beneath his shoulders broad.

It may have seemed a little remarkable that the 'wild genius' should so abound in classical allusions while the scholar poet was so free from them. But this would surprise no one who was familiar with the works of both; nor is it the most important difference. It is, in the logical sense, an accident that the figures which fill Shakespeare's description should come from classical mythology. It is their presence and their function, not their source, that matters. The two passages illustrate two radically different methods of poetical description. Milton keeps his eye on the

---

[1] It was between the 21st and the 30th.

M

object, and builds up his picture in what seems a natural order. It is distinguished from a prose catalogue largely by the verse, and by the exquisite choice not of the rarest words but of the words which will seem the most nobly obvious when once they have been chosen. 'Fair large front'—any one, you would say, could think of that. And yet how well it does its work. Those three monosyllables, heavy yet easily uttered, with the glorious vowel of *large*, have already smuggled into our minds the sense of massive, leisurely dignity: it is Michelangelo's Adam 'in that majestic indolence so dear to native man'; we are prepared for the words 'absolute rule' in the next line. Shakespeare's method is wholly different. Where Milton marches steadily forward, Shakespeare behaves rather like a swallow. He darts at the subject and glances away; and then he is back again before your eyes can follow him. It is as if he kept on having tries at it, and being dissatisfied. He darts image after image at you and still seems to think that he has not done enough. He brings up a whole light artillery of mythology, and gets tired of each piece almost before he has fired it. He wants to see the object from a dozen different angles; if the undignified word is pardonable, he *nibbles*, like a man trying a tough biscuit now from this side and now from that. You can find the same sort of contrast almost anywhere between these two poets. When Milton wishes to convey to us the greatness of Beelzebub he says:

> and in his rising seemed
> A pillar of state. Deep on his front engraven

Deliberation sat and public care,
And princely counsel in his face yet shone
Majestic, though in ruin. Sage he stood
With Atlantean shoulders, fit to bear
The weight of mightiest monarchies. His look
Drew audience and attention still as night
Or summer's noontide air.

But when Cleopatra wants to tell of Antony's greatness, she talks like this:

His legs bestrid the ocean: his rear'd arm
Crested the world: his voice was propertied
As all the tuned spheres, and that to friends;
But when he meant to quail and shake the orb
He was as rattling thunder. For his bounty
There was no winter in't: an autumn 'twas
That grew the more by reaping. His delights
Were dolphin like: they show'd his back above
The element they lived in, &c.

You see again how simple, how all of one piece, like the clean growth of a tulip, the Milton is: how diversified—more like a chrysanthemum—is the Shakespeare. In Milton you have first the visual impression; then the moral showing through it; the allusion to Atlas, so obvious that any one (we feel) could have guessed it was coming: finally the stillness, compared, so obviously, so un-cleverly, to night or noon, and yet doing to perfection the work it was meant to do. In Shakespeare, as before, you have the ends of the earth all brought together. You begin with the gigantic hyperbole of a man bestriding the ocean, or an arm cresting the world; you go on to the music of the spheres, to thunder, to the seasons, to dolphins. Nor does one image grow out of another. The arm cresting the world is not a development of the legs bestriding the ocean; it is *idem in alio*, a second attempt at the very same idea, an alternative. The dolphin idea is not a continuation of the autumn idea. It is a fresh start. He begins over again in every second line. If you extract the bare logical skeleton, the prose 'meaning' of each image, you will find that it is precisely the same in most of them. That is not so with the Milton: the prose abstract would take nearly as many words as the poetical expression. 'Beelzebub was very big; he looked wise; he looked wise though broken; his shoulders were broad; the people were hushed when they saw him.' If you do the same to Cleopatra's speech you get something like this: 'He was great. He was great. He was great enough to help his friends. He was great enough to hurt his enemies. He was generous. He was generous. He was great.' In short, Milton gives you a theme developing: Shakespeare plays variations on a theme that remains the same. In the one, touch after touch is added to the picture until the whole stands completed; in the other you get rather a series of lightning sketches, each of the same subject, and each tossed aside before the sketcher has really finished. We might distinguish these as the method of *construction* and the method of *variation*. The first does one thing as well as it can and then proceeds to the next; the second cannot do even one thing except by doing it several times, as if even one thing were inexhaustible, and the poet could only go on having shots at it until mere necessity forced him to give it up.

It would be a mistake to suppose that what we have here stumbled on is simply the difference between epic and dramatic poetry. If I could presume on endless patience I could show you the opposite. I could take Shakespeare where he is himself handling epic matter and show that the very same difference holds between him and Homer as between him and Milton. I would put the Prologue to the third Act of *Henry V*, where Phoebus is fanning the silken streamers and a city is dancing on the billows beside Homer's picture of the Greeks advancing 'in silence with their eyes upon their captains'. I would put a dozen speeches from ancient tragedy beside a dozen speeches from Shakespeare. Everywhere almost, though not everywhere to the same degree, we should find the same distinction.

Nor is the difference that between classical and romantic art. Milton's Beelzebub with his dim vastness and his ruined splendour is ten times more romantic than Cleopatra's Antony, whose greatness, under all its metaphorical deck hamper, remains greatness of a very mundane and lucrative type. The point can easily be settled by another example. Mr. Yeats says, of the fairies,

How shall I name you, immortal, mild, proud shadows?
I only know that all we know comes from you.

Prospero tackles them more like this

                   you demi puppets that
By moonshine do the green sour ringlets make
Whereof the ewe not bites, and you whose pastime
Is to make midnight mushrooms, that delight
To hear the solemn curfew.

Here both passages are utterly romantic; but they
are as different as any other two that I have cited.
Yeats gets his effect by packing as much mystery and
longing as he can into a single phrase, without figures:
Shakespeare, as always, flits from point to point, and
will have five or six attempts to make you see the
fairies, by catching them in different places. The
method of variation is not a characteristic either of
dramatic, or of romantic poetry. Still less is it peculiar
to Shakespeare. It is shared by all the Elizabethan
dramatists. It was there before Shakespeare.

> I will be Paris, and for love of thee
> Instead of Troy shall Wertenberg be sacked,
> And I will combat with weak Menelaus
> And wear thy colours on my plumed crest;
> Yea, I will wound Achilles in the heel
> And then return to Helen for a kiss.

If we reduce the prose content of this to 'I love you
well enough to fight for you, as Paris for Helen,' we
have still not done enough. For the Paris and Helen
idea is itself merely illustration, and the whole of
the rest of the passage is a ringing of the changes on
Paris and Helen, who themselves but ring the changes
on the original theme. The method is used equally
by a poet who piques himself on being different from
the general, like Ben Jonson. Thus in *Every Man in
his Humour*[1] I read

> Who will not judge him worthy to be robbed
> That sets his doors wide open to a thief
> And shews the felon where his treasure lies?
> Again what earthy spirit but will attempt

[1] Q. 1601, III. i.

To taste the fruit of beauty's golden tree
When leaden sleep seals up the dragon's eyes?
Oh beauty is a project of some power
Chiefly when opportunity attends her.
She will infuse true motion in a stone,
Put glowing fire in an icy soul,
Stuff peasants' bosoms with proud Caesar's spleen,
Pour rich device into an empty brain, &c.

The whole passage may very profitably be compared
with Milton's imitation of it in *Comus*. The six lines
beginning 'Oh beauty is a project', which contain
four distinct metaphorical expressions of precisely
the same idea, he throws out altogether. He keeps
the dragon idea, and the stores spread out in the
sight of a thief, but reverses the order. The dragon
comes first and is used for a different purpose. The
marvellous line 'Of dragon watch with unenchanted
eye' is the central phrase, and the metaphor as a
whole becomes less a rhetorical illustration of the
theme than an escape into pure imagination. The
hoard-and-thief idea is separated from it by the
words 'You may as well', and has the effect of
summing up the previous argument. It is not simply
one more point that has occurred to the speaker; it
is a return to the person addressed, as if he had
rounded on him.

It is the same with the later dramatists. If we ever
fail to notice it, it is because we are so used to it that
it comes to us merged in the general atmosphere of
'Elizabethan play'. 'Gentle father, To you I have
unclasped my burdened soul, Emptied the storehouse of my thoughts and heart, Made myself poor

of secrets: have not left Another word untold which
hath not spoke All that I ever durst or think or
know.'¹ Here are four variations on the theme 'I
have confided in you'. There is no movement.
Unclasping the burdened soul and emptying the
storehouse of one's thoughts are simply alternative
metaphors for the same idea. The one does not grow
out of the other, nor improve on it. Or again: 'You
dreamt of kingdoms, did ye? how to bosom The
delicacies of a youngling princess, How with this nod
to grace that subtle courtyer, How with that frown to
make this noble tremble.'² Here the variation is not
by metaphors, but, as we might say, by particulariza-
tion. You announce the theme of Kingship first and
then go on to ring the changes on particular aspects
of Kingship. It is one of the simplest ways of turning
an abstract conception into poetry, and is perhaps
the commonest of all forms of variation in these
dramatists. It does not differ essentially from the
metaphorical type. The same choice is before the
poet. Some abstraction is to be presented, say,
luxury, servility, folly. Are you to do it by finding
the single most suggestive phrase that you can and
then have done with it? Or are you to try to catch
a glimpse of it manifested in as many different modes
as you can and fling them all together, varying as
many aspects of the theme as possible? The Elizabethans nearly always chose the latter; often with
beautiful result.

> So shall the spirits of every element
> Be always serviceable to us three;

---

¹ *'Tis Pity She's a Whore*, I. i.   ² *The Broken Heart*, IV. iv.

Like lions shall they guard us when we please,
Like Almain rutters with their horseman's staves
Or Lapland giants trotting by our sides,
Sometimes like women or unwedded maids
Shadowing more beauty in their airy brows
Than have the white breasts of the queen of love.
From Venice shall they drag huge argosies
And from America the golden fleece.

That is Marlowe's way. The abstraction 'magical power' is turned into poetry by the process of variation—by offering you a handful of specimens. One is not enough for him; he tries it from this angle and from that. But there are other ways. Wordsworth has to express a much more abstract conception than that of magical power—the conception, namely, of restraints exercised upon the wiser sort of young men by the wrong sort of old men. He writes simply

> And blind authority beating with his staff
> The child that might have led him,

and the thing is done. We can all guess how the Elizabethans would have dealt with it. We should have begun, perhaps, with a flourish about authority in the abstract, old and sour as Saturn, but blind as Cupid; and then we should certainly have passed into a series of dissolving views in which we caught glimpses of authority at work—a man being progged in one line, and a conversation with a dean in the next.

It will be understood, of course, that variation occurs to some extent in all poetry whatsoever. What is the Hebrew parallelism but a kind of variation? The synonyms in Anglo-Saxon are the same. But

I think it is not likely to be disputed that the Elizabethan dramatists used it more extensively than any other family of poets. All poets use metaphors; all poets turn the abstract into the concrete; but if we want to see multiplication of metaphors about the same idea, and if we want to see concreteness given not by a single imaginative phrase but by multiplication of instances, then we naturally turn to Shakespeare and his neighbours. The faculty which enabled a man to practise such variation, which stocked his mind with images and which brought a riot of images tumbing over one another to greet every single idea was for the Elizabethans the essential faculty of the poet. They called it Wit. Middleton in his *Changeling*[1] writes:

> Love has an intellect that runs through all
> The scrutinous sciences and like a cunning poet
> Catches a quantity of every knowledge
> Yet brings all home into one mystery.

This may be taken simply as a description of that esemplastic power which is involved in all poetry. But it has a special meaning for the seventeenth century. Never were the scrutinous sciences and the quantities of every knowledge expected to lie quite so ready to the poet's hand; never were poets so eager to bring them *all* home (if it were possible) on every occasion.

It is no part of my purpose to compare this kind of writing with others. Whether you prefer the poetry which deals chiefly in construction or that which deals chiefly in variation is largely a matter of tem-

[1] III. iii. 131.

perament. Any sane man will want both. In Shirley
you may see this style in the last stages of its decay;
all its peculiar vices—for every method has its vices—
are then painfully visible. But it is more interesting
to consider what this practice of variation could do
at its best. What were the kingdoms of poetry which
it alone could conquer, and whose conquest made
it so dangerously attractive to the weaker poets?
To ask this is, of course, equivalent to asking what
Shakespeare did with it.

If we lay aside all the bardolatrous nonsense of
those who would have us believe that Shakespeare
was God or Nature, and ask what, in a few words,
was his distinctive contribution to poetry, I really do
not know why we should be afraid of answering the
question. The largest things ought to be the most
easily seen. The law of gravity is perhaps simpler
than the Law of Tort. It is the minor poets whose
quality is really indefinable, because it is nearly
nothing. Thus fortified I venture to submit that
the mark of Shakespeare (and it is quite enough for
one mortal man) is simply this; to have combined
two species of excellence which are not, in a remarkable degree, combined by any other artist, namely
the imaginative splendour of the highest type of
lyric and the realistic presentation of human life and
character. Pindar and Aeschylus and Keats are quite
as good as he on one side; and Jane Austen, Meredith,
and George Eliot can meet him on the other. But
Jane Austen could not write stuff like the choruses
in the *Agamemnon*, and Keats (judging by *Cap and
Bells*) would have made a poor show among the

Bennets and the Bingleys—(not such a very poor show, when you remember some of the passages in the letters). Now the possibility of combining two such diverse qualities depends precisely on the use of variation. The problem which Shakespeare solved, perhaps unconsciously, is a very difficult one. If the character speaks as living men speak, how are we to have in his language the revealing splendours of imagination? for real passion is not articulate. We must give his poetic metaphors the air of being thrown off accidentally as he gropes for expression in the very heat of dialogue. He must have a slight stammer in his thought, and his best things must not come at the first attempt. For on those rare occasions when real life finds the inevitable phrase, that is how it arises. The man fumbles and returns again and again to his theme, and hardly knows which of his words has really hit the mark. Listen to Hamlet:

> O that this too too solid flesh would melt—
> Thaw and resolve itself into a dew!
> Or that the Everlasting had not fixed
> His canon 'gainst self slaughter. O God, God!
> How weary, stale, flat and unprofitable
> Seem to me all the uses of this world.
> Fie on't, ah fie! 'Tis an unweeded garden
> That grows to seed: things rank and gross in nature
> Possess it merely.

The flesh resolving itself into a dew, and the unweeded garden are poetical metaphors that, taken alone, might seem to come from the heights of fully wrought lyric, expressing real experience but not as life expresses it. If Hamlet used either of them he

would speak only as a poet. We should not believe
that a man spoke thus. We shall believe them only
if he seems to stumble upon them by accident, if
they come, as it were, spat out amid a chaos of other
grumbles as he chews over and over again the cud
of the same bitter experience. That is how Shakespeare claims for naturalistic poetry—the poetry of
the close up—all the rights of that other poetry which
sees its figures at a mythical distance. See how he
ballasts his imaginative phases with mere exclama-
tions—'O God, God!' and 'Fie on't, ah fie.' A
magnificent example of the same thing occurs in
Macbeth:

> Methought I heard a voice cry 'Sleep no more!
> Macbeth does murder sleep'—the innocent sleep,
> Sleep that knits up the ravell'd sleave of care,
> The death of each day's life, sore labour's bath,
> Balm of hurt minds, great nature's second course,
> Chief nourisher in life's feast.

Here the metaphors are perhaps even more highly
wrought than Hamlet's. If Macbeth had said only
'sleep that knits up the ravell'd sleave of care', he
would have said one of the best things that have
been said of sleep. But we should not have believed
It is art, not life, that selects from the mind's chaos
the one 'predestined and elected phrase That had
lain bound long nights and days Until it wore
when once set free Immortal pellucidity'. It is the
very fact that Macbeth will not leave it at that which
carries conviction. Because he is not writing a poem
but blurting out the agony of his mind he has no
leisure to notice that he has said a good thing. The

words come tumbling one after the other, and it is only we the spectators, who gather them up and see that almost every sentence has been a poem in itself. We conclude—and this goes to the root of the matter— that Macbeth was a great poet. It is only in Shakespeare's plays that we call the characters, as well as the author, poets. No one describes Clytemnestra as a poet. The poetry belongs to Aeschylus. We know that a real Clytemnestra would not talk like that. It is the poet, quite legitimately, who puts into her mouth the language she would not, in real life, have used, and thereby enables us to see her character more luminously than real life would have allowed us to see it. But Shakespeare makes you believe that Othello and Macbeth really spoke as we hear them speak. Without sacrificing the splendour, he has kept the lower and more factual reality as well; it is the very marriage of the mimetic and the creative, and it can hardly be done except by variation.

It would be untrue, however, to say that Shakespeare always used variation to such good purpose. Very often, and specially in his earlier work, he uses it as a poetical ornament—to decorate, and not to render more real, the dramatic situation.

> His rash fierce blase of riot cannot last,
> For violent fires soon burn out themselves;
> Small showers last long but sudden storms are short;
> He tires betimes that spurs too fast betimes;
> With eager feeding food doth choke the feeder;
> Light vanity, insatiate cormorant,
> Consuming means, soon preys upon itself.

Here, the not very profound idea hardly requires

such a wealth of illustration, and we hardly believe that it would have received it. The passage comes trippingly off the tongue: it is written, I think, for the mere fun of the thing. Such examples are frequent in the earlier plays, and it is in these passages that Shakespeare reminds us most strongly of Marlowe; Marlowe who of all others used variation with the minimum of dramatic purpose, and the maximum of musical and rhetorical effect.

> Cut is the branch that might have grown full straight
> And burned is Apollo's laurel bough.

In Shakespeare the variations are either ornament, or else, as we have seen, a method of combining poetry and realism. In Shirley they are a recipe for poetry. I do not mean that he uses the figure more constantly than his predecessors; I mean that when he is not using it he has commonly no pretence of poetry. To mark a heightened moment, or to translate an abstract conception into something that looks like poetry, variation is his unfailing resource. When Shirley had jotted down what was to be covered in a given scene, the process of converting it into actual drama consisted either of those purely dramatic articulations in which he does not differ from the prose dramatist or in variation. Where there is poetry there is variation; where there is no variation there is no poetry. Consider the opening scene between Bornwell and his wife in *The Lady of Pleasure*. The theme can be stated in a few words. A husband rebukes his wife for extravagance and is obstinately answered. A real dramatist would have found in

this matter for as many pages as Shirley; but those
pages would have been occupied by the development in dialogue of the emotional situation between
the two characters. Every speech would have left
them related to each other in a slightly new way.
On the other hand a pure poet, of the constructive
type, would have given us in some few unforgettable
words an image clearer than life of the essential
quality of luxury and extravagance. We should have
seen once and for all what prodigality in all its
wasteful beauty means to the imagination. A single
line might do it, such as Clytemnestra's

Ἔστιν θάλασσα, τίς δέ νιν κατασβέσει;
Who shall quench all the purple of the sea?

A writer who was both a poet and a dramatist would
have given us both together. Every speech would
have added a new quality to the relation of the
speakers and at the same time would have done
what Aeschylus does. Shirley's method is different
from either. On the strictly dramatic side he has
nothing to say that could not have been said in six
lines. 'Why are you angry?' asks Bornwell. 'Because
you stint me,' retorts the lady. 'I don't. On the
contrary I allow you to spend far too much,' says
Bornwell. 'Well, I still think you're mean,' says Lady
Bornwell. That is the whole scene, as drama. What
swells it to its. 130 odd lines is pure *variation* on the
theme 'you spend too much' put into the mouth of
Bornwell. During this the dramatic situation stands
still. 'Have you done, Sir?' Lady Bornwell asks at the
end of her husband's first speech; at the end of his
third she is still asking, 'Have you concluded your

lecture?' The angry husband and the scornful wife remain dramatically immobile and the play ceases to go forward while the waves of variation roll over the audience. In other words, what Shirley has here to say as a dramatist is extremely little; and to convert that little into something that should seem richer he has to call in variation. The variation consists, of course, simply of an endless string of examples of the lady's extravagance—'this Italian master and that Dutchman', 'superfluous plate', 'vanities of tires', 'petticoats and pearls'. There is no reason why any one image should stand where it does rather than elsewhere. There is no reason why the thing should stop where it does: you might just as well turn the tap off twenty lines sooner or twenty lines later. Nor does the beauty of the separate items recompense us (as it would in Marlowe) for their lack of definite tendency. The best that such writing can do is to give us a vague impression of an angry man who has a great deal to say; but it does this only by making him as tedious as he would be in real life. No method could be easier for the writer; any one who can scan a verse and has a memory well stored can produce such work *ad libitum*. And as if this were not enough the scene between Bornwell and his wife is followed almost immediately by the similar scene between Celestina and her steward. Here, once again, the theme is extravagance opposed to frugality; once again the dramatic development, such as it is, could be shown in a few lines; all the rest is variation. In the next act we have the arrival of Master Frederick and Lady Bornwell's disgust at his scholarly lack of

N

fashion. Here is a situation very recalcitrant to
poetical treatment, but very tempting to a real comic
dramatist. It would go admirably into a prose
dialogue of short questions and replies. Everything
ought to be on the move. We ought to see Lady
Bornwell's gradual discovery of her nephew's character and opinions: the rift ought to widen at every
speech, and at every speech the audience ought to
perceive more exactly just what the rift is and how
comically exasperating. Instead of this, Shirley lets
Lady Bornwell grasp the whole truth, beyond hope
of error, and express her horror, in the very first line,
'Support me, I shall faint'. The suddenness of this
is not without its comic effect; but it is dearly pur-
chased at the price of the following scene, in which,
dramatically speaking, there is nothing left to do.
The chasm is filled up as usual by the handy rubble
of variation. Lady Bornwell's long speech is merely
a string of variations on the theme 'I wish he were
French and fashionable instead of studious and par-
sonical', which is itself only an unprogressive amplifi-
cation of the opening words 'I shall faint'. And
Frederick replies:

> Madam, with your pardon, you have practised
> Another dialect than was taught me when
> I was commended to your care and breeding.
> I understand not this. Latin or Greek
> Are more familiar to my apprehension.
> Logic was not so hard in my first lectures
> As your strange language.

The whole speech is variation; and even the theme
which it varies, namely the theme 'My ways are

conditions of Shakespeare's peculiar greatness. I do not, however, believe that Shakespeare consciously selected the method as a means to that combination of the dramatic and the poetic in which its greatest potential virtue lies. His own early use of it is purely ornamental, and this suggests that he began by accepting it from tradition without much reflection. Its origins, so far as I know, have not been fully examined. I suppose them to lie in Medieval Latin literature of the rhetorical type. A new study of that literature with special reference to its influence on the vernacular poets of what is called the 'Renaissance', and a determined inquiry into the channels by which that influence reached them, would be a very useful work.

IX

CHRISTIANITY AND LITERATURE

'Ο τοῦ θεοῦ λόγος, λύραν μὲν καὶ κιθάραν ὑπεριδών, κόσμον δὲ τόνδε
καὶ δὴ καὶ τὸν σμικρὸν κόσμον, τὸν ἄνθρωπον, ψυχήν τε καὶ σῶμα
αὐτοῦ, ἁγίῳ πνεύματι ἁρμοσάμενος, ψάλλει τῷ θεῷ . . . καλὸν ὁ
κύριος ὄργανον ἔμπνουν τὸν ἄνθρωπον ἐξειργάσατο κατ' εἰκόνα τὴν
ἑαυτοῦ· ἀμέλει καὶ αὐτὸς ὄργανόν ἐστι τοῦ θεοῦ παναρμόνιον.

CLEMENT OF ALEXANDRIA, *Protrepticos*, i.

The Divine Word, not with harp and lyre, but rather tuning
as His instrument, by the Holy Spirit, this whole world and
the little world of man, both soul and body, makes music
before God. A sweet and lively instrument Our Lord makes
of man, and one like Himself: for certainly He also is God's
instrument of music, all-harmonious.

A peal
Of laughter, all the angels crying *You!*
Here is a fellow calls himself I.

CHARLES WILLIAMS

Read to a religious society at Oxford

CHRISTIANITY AND LITERATURE

WHEN I was asked to address this society, I was at first tempted to refuse because the subject proposed to me, that of Christianity and Literature, did not seem to admit of any discussion. I knew, of course, that Christian story and sentiment were among the things on which literature could be written, and, conversely, that literature was one of the ways in which Christian sentiment could be expressed and Christian story told; but there seemed nothing more to be said of Christianity in this connexion than of any of the hundred and one other things that men made books about. We are familiar, no doubt, with the expression 'Christian Art', by which people usually mean Art that represents Biblical or hagiological scenes, and there is, in this sense, a fair amount of 'Christian Literature'. But I question whether it has any literary qualities peculiar to itself. The rules for writing a good passion play or a good devotional lyric are simply the rules for writing tragedy or lyric in general: success in sacred literature depends on the same qualities of structure, suspense, variety, diction, and the like which secure success in secular literature. And if we enlarge the idea of Christian Literature to include not only literature on sacred themes but all that is written by Christians for Christians to read, then, I think, Christian Literature can exist only in the same sense in which Christian cookery might exist. It would be possible, and it might be edifying, to write a Christian cookery book. Such a book would exclude dishes whose preparation

involves unnecessary human labour or animal suffering, and dishes excessively luxurious. That is to say, its
choice of dishes would be Christian. But there could
be nothing specifically Christian about the actual
cooking of the dishes included. Boiling an egg is the
same process whether you are a Christian or a Pagan.
In the same way, literature written by Christians
for Christians would have to avoid mendacity,
cruelty, blasphemy, pornography, and the like, and
it would aim at edification in so far as edification
was proper to the kind of work in hand. But whatever it chose to do would have to be done by the
means common to all literature; it could succeed or
fail only by the same excellences and the same faults
as all literature; and its literary success or failure
would never be the same thing as its obedience or
disobedience to Christian principles.

I have been speaking so far of Christian Literature
proprement dite—that is, of writing which is intended
to affect us as literature, by its appeal to imagination.
But in the visible arts I think we can make a distinction between sacred art, however sacred in theme,
and pure iconography—between that which is intended, in the first instance, to affect the imagination
and the aesthetic appetite, and that which is meant
merely as the starting-point for devotion and medi-
tation. If I were treating the visible arts I should
have to work out here a full distinction of the work
of art from the icon on the one hand and the toy on
the other. The icon and the toy have this in common
that their value depends very little on their perfection
as artefacts—a shapeless rag may give as much

pleasure as the costliest doll, and two sticks tied crosswise may kindle as much devotion as the work of Leonardo. And to make matters more complicated the very same object could often be used in all three ways. But I do not think the icon and the work of art can be so sharply distinguished in literature. I question whether the badness of a really bad hymn can ordinarily be so irrelevant to devotion as the badness of a bad devotional picture. Because the hymn uses words, its badness will, to some degree, consist in confused or erroneous thought and unworthy sentiment. But I mention this difficult question here only to say that I do not propose to treat it. If any literary works exist which have a purely iconographic value and no literary value, they are not what I am talking about. Indeed I could not, for I have not met them.

Of Christian Literature, then, in the sense of 'work aiming at literary value and written by Christians for Christians', you see that I have really nothing to say and believe that nothing can be said. But I think I have something to say about what may be called the Christian approach to literature: about the principles, if you will, of Christian literary theory and criticism. For while I was thinking over the subject you gave me I made what seemed to me a discovery. It is not an easy one to put into words. The nearest I can come to it is to say that I found a disquieting contrast between the whole circle of ideas used in modern criticism and certain ideas recurrent in the New Testament. Let me say at once that it is hardly a question of logical contradiction between clearly defined concepts. It is too vague for that. It is more a repugnance of atmospheres, a discordance of notes, an incompatibility of temperaments.

What are the key-words of modern criticism? *Creative*, with its opposite *derivative*; *spontaneity*, with its opposite *convention*; *freedom*, contrasted with *rules*. Great authors are innovators, pioneers, explorers; bad authors bunch in schools and follow models. Or again, great authors are always 'breaking fetters' and 'bursting bonds'. They have personality, they 'are themselves'. I do not know whether we often think out the implication of such language into a consistent philosophy; but we certainly have a general picture of bad work flowing from conformity and discipleship, and of good work bursting out from certain centres of explosive force—apparently self-originating force— which we call men of genius.

Now the New Testament has nothing at all to tell us of literature. I know that there are some who like to think of Our Lord Himself as a poet and cite the parables to support their view. I admit freely that to believe in the Incarnation at all is to believe that every mode of human excellence is implicit in His historical human character: poethood, of course, included. But if all had been developed, the limitations of a single human life would have been transcended and He would not have been a man; therefore all excellences save the spiritual remained in varying degrees implicit. If it is claimed that the poetic excellence is more developed than others—say, the intellectual—I think I deny the claim. Some of the parables do work like poetic similes; but then others work like philosophic illustrations. Thus the Unjust Judge is not emotionally or imaginatively like God: he corresponds to God as the terms in a proportion correspond, because he is to the Widow (in one highly specialized respect) as God is to man. In that parable Our Lord, if we may so express it, is much more like Socrates than Shakespeare. And I dread an over-emphasis on the poetical element in His words because I think it tends to obscure that quality in His human character which is, in fact, so visible in His irony, His *argumenta ad homines*, and His use of the *a fortiori*, and which I would call the homely, peasant shrewdness. Donne points out that we are never told He laughed; it is difficult in reading the Gospels not to believe, and to tremble in believing, that He smiled.

I repeat, the New Testament has nothing to say of literature; but what it says on other subjects is quite sufficient to strike that note which I find out of tune with the language of modern criticism. I must begin with something that is unpopular. St. Paul tells us (1 Cor. xi. 3) that man is the 'head' of woman. We may soften this if we like by saying that he means only man *quâ* man and woman *quâ* woman and that an equality of the sexes as citizens or intellectual beings is not therefore absolutely repugnant to his thought: indeed, that he himself tells us that in another respect, that is 'in the Lord', the sexes cannot be thus separated (ibid. v. 11). But what concerns me here is to find out what he means by Head. Now in verse 3 he has given us a very remarkable proportion sum: that God is to Christ as

Christ is to man and man is to woman, and the relation between each term and the next is that of Head.
And in verse 7 we are told that man is God's image
and glory, and woman is man's glory. He does not
repeat 'image', but I question whether the omission is
intentional, and I suggest that we shall have a fairly
Pauline picture of this whole series of Head relations
running from God to woman if we picture each term
as the 'image and glory' of the preceding term. And
I suppose that of which one is the image and glory
is that which one glorifies by copying or imitating.
Let me once again insist that I am not trying to twist
St. Paul's metaphors into a logical system. I know
well that whatever picture he is building up, he himself will be the first to throw it aside when it has
served its turn and to adopt some quite different
picture when some new aspect of the truth is present
to his mind. But I want to see clearly the sort of
picture implied in this passage—to get it clear
however temporary its use or partial its application.
And it seems to me a quite clear picture; we are to
think of some original divine virtue passing down-
wards from rung to rung of a hierarchical ladder,
and the mode in which each lower rung receives it
is, quite frankly, imitation.

What is perhaps most startling in this picture is
the apparent equivalence of the woman-man and
man-God relation with the relation between Christ
and God, or, in Trinitarian language, with the
relation between the First and Second Persons of the
Trinity. As a layman and a comparatively recently
reclaimed apostate I have, of course, no intention

of building a theological system—still less of setting up a *catena* of New Testament metaphors as a criticism on the Nicene or the Athanasian creed, documents which I wholly accept. But it is legitimate to notice what kinds of metaphor the New Testament uses; more especially when what we are in search of is not dogma but a kind of flavour or atmosphere. And there is no doubt that this kind of proportion sum—A : B : : B : C—is quite freely used in the New Testament where A and B represent the First and Second Persons of the Trinity. Thus St. Paul has already told us earlier in the same epistle that we are 'of Christ' and Christ is 'of God' (iii. 23). Thus again in the Fourth Gospel, Our Lord Himself compares the relation of the Father to the Son with that of the Son to His flock, in respect of knowledge (x. 15) and of love (xv. 9).

I suggest, therefore, that this picture of a hierarchical order in which we are encouraged—though, of course, only from certain points of view and in certain respects—to regard the Second Person Himself as a step, or stage, or degree, is wholly in accord with the spirit of the New Testament. And if we ask how the stages are connected the answer always seems to be something like imitation, reflection, assimilation. Thus in Gal. iv. 19 Christ is to be 'formed' inside each believer—the verb here used ($\mu o\rho\phi\omega\theta\hat{\eta}$) meaning to shape, to figure, or even to draw a sketch. In First Thessalonians (i. 6) Christians are told to imitate St. Paul and the Lord, and elsewhere (1 Cor. x. 33) to imitate St. Paul as he in his turn imitates Christ— thus giving us another stage of progressive imitation.

Changing the metaphor we find that believers are to acquire the fragrance of Christ, *redolere Christum* (2 Cor. ii. 16): that the glory of God has appeared in the face of Christ as, at the creation, light appeared in the universe (2 Cor. iv. 6); and, finally, if my reading of a much disputed passage is correct, that a Christian is to Christ as a mirror to an object (2 Cor. iii. 18).

These passages, you will notice, are all Pauline; but there is a place in the Fourth Gospel which goes much farther—so far that if it were not a Dominical utterance we would not venture to think along such lines. There (v. 19) we are told that the Son does only what He sees the Father doing. He watches the Father's operations and does the same (ὁμοίως ποιεῖ) or 'copies'. The Father, because of His love for the Son, shows Him all that He does. I have already explained that I am not a theologian. What aspect of the Trinitarian reality Our Lord, as God, saw while He spoke these words, I do not venture to define; but I think we have a right and even a duty to notice carefully the earthly image by which He expressed it—to see clearly the picture He puts before us. It is a picture of a boy learning to do things by watching a man at work. I think we may even guess what memory, humanly speaking, was in His mind. It is hard not to imagine that He remembered His boyhood, that He saw Himself as a boy in a carpenter's shop, a boy learning how to do things by watching while St. Joseph did them. So taken, the passage does not seem to me to conflict with anything I have learned from the creeds, but greatly to enrich my conception of the Divine sonship.

Now it may be that there is no absolute logical contradiction between the passages I have quoted and the assumptions of modern criticism: but I think there is so great a difference of temper that a man whose mind was at one with the mind of the New Testament would not, and indeed could not, fall into the language which most critics now adopt. In the New Testament the art of life itself is an art of imitation: can we, believing this, believe that literature, which must derive from real life, is to aim at being 'creative', 'original', and 'spontaneous'. 'Originality' in the New Testament is quite plainly the prerogative of God alone; even within the triune being of God it seems to be confined to the Father. The duty and happiness of every other being is placed in being derivative, in reflecting like a mirror. Nothing could be more foreign to the tone of scripture than the language of those who describe a saint as a 'moral genius' or a 'spiritual genius' thus insinuating that his virtue or spirituality is 'creative' or 'original'. If I have read the New Testament aright, it leaves no room for 'creativeness' even in a modified or metaphorical sense. Our whole destiny seems to lie in the opposite direction, in being as little as possible ourselves, in acquiring a fragrance that is not our own but borrowed, in becoming clean mirrors filled with the image of a face that is not ours. I am not here supporting the doctrine of total depravity, and I do not say that the New Testament supports it; I am saying only that the highest good of a creature must be creaturely—that is, derivative or reflective—good. In other words, as St. Augustine makes plain (*De. Civ.*

Dei xii, cap 1), pride does not only go before a fall but is a fall—a fall of the creature's attention from what is better, God, to what is worse, itself.

Applying this principle to literature, in its greatest generality, we should get as the basis of all critical theory the maxim that an author should never conceive himself as bringing into existence beauty or wisdom which did not exist before, but simply and solely as trying to embody in terms of his own art some reflection of eternal Beauty and Wisdom. Our criticism would therefore from the beginning group itself with some existing theories of poetry against others. It would have affinities with the primitive or Homeric theory in which the poet is the mere pensioner of the Muse. It would have affinities with the Platonic doctrine of a transcendent Form partly imitable on earth; and remoter affinities with the Aristotelian doctrine of μίμησις and the Augustan doctrine about the imitation of Nature and the Ancients. It would be opposed to the theory of genius as, perhaps, generally understood; and above all it would be opposed to the idea that literature is self-expression.

But here some distinctions must be made. I spoke just now of the ancient idea that the poet was merely the servant of some god, of Apollo, or the Muse; but let us not forget the highly paradoxical words in which Homer's Phemius asserts his claim to be a poet—

Αὐτοδίδακτος δ' εἰμί, θεὸς δέ μοι ἐν φρεσὶν οἴμας
Παντοίας ἐνέφυσεν. (*Od.* xxii. 347.)

'I am self-taught; a god has inspired me with all

manner of songs.' It sounds like a direct contradiction. How can he be self-taught if the god has
taught him all he knows? Doubtless because the
god's instruction is given internally, not through the
senses, and is therefore regarded as part of the Self,
to be contrasted with such external aids as, say, the
example of other poets, And this seems to blur the
distinction I am trying to draw between Christian
imitation and the 'originality' praised by modern
critics. Phemius obviously claims to be original, in
the sense of being no other poet's disciple, and in the
same breath admits his complete dependence on a
supernatural teacher. Does not this let in 'originality' and 'creativeness' of the only kind that have
ever been claimed?

If you said 'the only kind that ought to have been
claimed', I would agree; but as things are, I think
the distinction remains, though it becomes finer than
our first glance suggested. A Christian and an un-
believing poet may both be equally original in the
sense that they neglect the example of their poetic
forbears and draw on resources peculiar to themselves, but with this difference. The unbeliever may
take his own temperament and experience, just as
they happen to stand, and consider them worth com-
municating simply because they are facts or, worse
still, because they are his. To the Christian his own
temperament and experience, as mere fact, and as
merely his, are of no value or importance whatsoever: he will deal with them, if at all, only because
they are the medium through which, or the position from which, something universally profitable

o

appeared to him. We can imagine two men seated in different parts of a church or theatre. Both, when they come out, may tell us their experiences, and both may use the first person. But the one is interested in his seat only because it was his—'I was most uncomfortable,' he will say. 'You would hardly believe what a draught comes in from the door in that corner. And the people! I had to speak pretty sharply to the woman in front of me.' The other will tell us what could be seen from his seat, choosing to describe this because this is what he knows, and because every seat must give the best view of something. 'Do you know', he will begin, 'the moulding on those pillars goes on round at the back. It looks, too, as if the design on the back were the older of the two.' Here we have the expressionist and the Christian attitudes towards the self or temperament. Thus St. Augustine and Rousseau both write *Confessions*; but to the one his own temperament is a kind of absolute (*au moins je suis autre*), to the other it is 'a narrow house, too narrow for Thee to enter—oh make it wide. It is in ruins—oh rebuild it.' And Wordsworth, the romantic who made a good end, has a foot in either world and though he practises both, distinguishes well the two ways in which a man may be said to write about himself. On the one hand he says:

> I must tread on shadowy ground, must sink
> Deep, and aloft ascending breathe in worlds
> To which the heaven of heavens is but a veil.

On the other he craves indulgence if

>   with this
> I mix more lowly matter; with the thing

Contemplated, describe the Mind and Man
Contemplating; and who and what he was—
The transitory being that beheld
This vision.

In this sense, then, the Christian writer may be
self-taught or original. He may base his work on the
'transitory being' that he is, not because he thinks
it valuable (for he knows that in his flesh dwells no
good thing), but solely because of the 'vision' that
appeared to it. But he will have no preference for
doing this. He will do it if it happens to be the thing
he can do best; but if his talents are such that he
can produce good work by writing in an established
form and dealing with experiences common to all
his race, he will do so just as gladly. I even think he
will do so more gladly. It is to him an argument
not of strength but of weakness that he should respond fully to the vision only 'in his own way'. And
always, of every idea and of every method he will ask
not 'Is it mine?', but 'Is it good?'

This seems to me the most fundamental difference
between the Christian and the unbeliever in their
approach to literature. But I think there is another.
The Christian will take literature a little less seriously
than the cultured Pagan: he will feel less uneasy with
a purely hedonistic standard for at least many kinds
of work. The unbeliever is always apt to make a kind
of religion of his aesthetic experiences; he feels
ethically irresponsible, perhaps, but he braces his
strength to receive responsibilities of another kind
which seem to the Christian quite illusory. He has
to be 'creative'; he has to obey a mystical amoral

law called his artistic conscience; and he commonly
wishes to maintain his superiority to the great mass
of mankind who turn to books for mere recreation.
But the Christian knows from the outset that the
salvation of a single soul is more important than the
production or preservation of all the epics and
tragedies in the world: and as for superiority, he
knows that the vulgar since they include most of the
poor probably include most of his superiors. He has
no objection to comedies that merely amuse and
tales that merely refresh; for he thinks like Thomas
Aquinas *ipsa ratio hoc habet ut quandoque rationis usus
intercipiatur*. We can play, as we can eat, to the glory
of God. It thus may come about that Christian
views on literature will strike the world as shallow
and flippant; but the world must not misunderstand. When Christian work is done on a serious
subject there is no gravity and no sublimity it cannot
attain. But they will belong to the theme. That is
why they will be real and lasting—mighty nouns
with which literature, an adjectival thing, is here
united, far over-topping the fussy and ridiculous
claims of literature that tries to be important simply
as literature. And *a posteriori* it is not hard to argue
that all the greatest poems have been made by men
who valued something else much more than poetry—
even if that something else were only cutting down
enemies in a cattle-raid or tumbling a girl in a bed.
The real frivolity, the solemn vacuity, is all with
those who make literature a self-existent thing to be
valued for its own sake. Pater prepared for pleasure
as if it were martyrdom.

Now that I see where I have arrived a doubt assails me. It all sounds suspiciously like things I have said before, starting from very different premisses. Is it King Charles's Head? Have I mistaken for the 'vision' the same old 'transitory being' who, in some ways, is not nearly transitory enough? It may be so: or I may, after all, be right. I would rather be right if I could; but if not, if I have only been once more following my own footprints, it is the sort of tragi-comedy which, on my own principles, I must try to enjoy. I find a beautiful example proposed in the *Paradiso* (xxviii) where poor Pope Gregory, arrived in Heaven, discovered that his theory of the hier-archies, on which presumably he had taken pains, was quite wrong. We are told how the redeemed soul behaved; '*di sè medesmo rise*'. It was the funniest thing he'd ever heard.